Gardening
FOR
DUMMIES®
POCKET EDITION

**by Steven A. Frowine
with the Editors of the National
Gardening Association**

WILEY

John Wiley & Sons, Inc.

Gardening For Dummies®, Pocket Edition

Published by
John Wiley & Sons, Inc.
111 River St.
Hoboken, NJ 07030-5774
www.wiley.com

Publisher's Acknowledgments

Senior Project Editor: Georgette Beatty
Composition Services: Indianapolis Composition Services Department
Cover Photo: © iStockphoto.com/Chris Price

WILEY

Table of Contents

Introduction

• •

*A*ren't you lucky! You're entering or are already part of the most popular and rewarding lifelong hobby that exists — worldwide. Gardening is a common language that knows no national, socioeconomic, or age boundaries. It's a common thread that binds all of us together. Whether you're discussing your outrageous zucchini harvest of the previous year or sharing your secret tips for prizewinning roses, you've probably found that gardeners have an instant bond, no matter what their level of experience.

Because gardening is a huge topic that encompasses a wide field of cultivation interests and disciplines, it's impossible for any one book to cover everything there is to know about gardening. However, when you're armed with the gardening basics, like those presented in this book, you're ready for just about anything that the art of gardening can throw at you.

About This Book

Following the classic *For Dummies* format, this book gives you the most basic gardening information you need, organized and presented in an easy-to-follow, modular manner. Although you can read from cover-to-cover, you don't have to. This book can function as a reference work, so you can jump in, find what you need, and get back to your stand of birch trees or the koi pond or the garden center or wherever else you'd like to be.

After reading this book, you may not be an expert, but you should be well on your way to taking on most gardening tasks with new confidence. Gardening is part science and part art, and how you mix them up is a very personal thing. After getting a handle on the basics presented here, you can move on to develop your own style and techniques that work best for you.

Conventions Used in This Book

As you advance in gardening, you find that in certain branches of horticulture (like perennials), you're confronted with dreaded scientific names (usually Latin, sometimes Greek). People use such names in these plant categories for very legitimate reasons, and you can choose to follow the path to those reasons later. For now, I spare you that step by mostly using common names for the plants throughout this book. When I do provide the scientific name, I give common plant names first, followed by the botanical name.

As is typical of all *For Dummies* books, I also shy away from as much jargon as possible, and I explain any terms used right away (often in parentheses following the term). New, defined terms may also appear in *italics.* Horticulture and gardening can be as technical as any other science, but this is not a textbook for Horticulture 101!

The Internet is part of life now and can provide oodles of great gardening information, so I include various Web references. Web addresses appear in `monofont`. When this book was printed, some Web addresses may have needed to break across two lines of text. If that happened, rest assured that I haven't put in any extra characters (such as hyphens) to indicate the break. When using one of these Web addresses, just type in exactly what you see in this book, pretending as though the line break weren't there.

What You're Not to Read

If you're short on time and just want to get down to the nitty-gritty, you can skip the stuff in the gray boxes. I include this sidebar information for those of you who want to know the *whys* of everything or who just want to dig deeper.

Foolish Assumptions

Because you're reading this book, I assume that, like me, you really love gardening. Here are some other things I assume regarding your possible background:

- ✔ You've seen other folks' gardens that have inspired you, so now you want to bring your own gardening skill to the next level.
- ✔ You're concerned about a healthy diet and want to grow some of your own vegetables.
- ✔ You love outdoor living and you want to improve the space around you.
- ✔ You like the idea of gardening but don't know where to start.

Icons Used in This Book

Icons are the cute little pictures that show up in the margins of the book, right next to certain blocks of text. Here's what those icons stand for:

Gardeners sometimes speak their own lingo, which can be a bit confusing for people who are just getting their feet wet (or dirty) in the gardening process. This icon helps to identify and clarify the most common terms.

 This icon points out some major ideas in the book — stuff well worth remembering.

 The *Tip* icon flags notable gardening information that even experienced gardeners may not know. This info can save you time and frustration.

 This icon alerts you to possible problems to watch out for or avoid. These problems may result in injury or at the very least a bad gardening experience.

Where to Go from Here

You've got your Pocket Edition of *Gardening For Dummies* — now what? This pocket guide is a reference, so if you need information on planning your garden, head to Chapter 2. Or if you're interested in finding out about growing vegetables, go straight to Chapter 6. Or heck, start with Chapter 1 and read the chapters in order . . . you rebel. If you want even more advice on gardening, from growing annuals and perennials to the gear you need, check out the full-size version of *Gardening Basics For Dummies* — simply head to your local book seller or go to www. dummies.com!

Chapter 1

Getting Ready for Gardening

● ●

In This Chapter

▶ Understanding how plants are named

▶ Examining flowering plants

● ●

*N*o matter what your main gardening interest — be it growing vegetables or making your yard colorful with flowers — chances are that you care most about the plants. Sure, gardening can also involve landscaping and lawn care, or just having a great excuse to play in the dirt, but for most people, the plants make everything worthwhile.

Of course, keeping your plants alive and making them look their best involves a lot of preparation. This book contains information on caring for your garden plants throughout, but you should especially read through the first few chapters if you really want your plants to grow, thrive, and look their absolute best.

Okay, yeah, I know, you already know you need to plan and prepare your soil to get your garden going, but you *really* just want to read about plants right now, right? In that case, this chapter is devoted to the most basic explanations of some kinds of plants you may encounter in the world of gardening. First, though, I explain a bit about names.

Playing the Name Game

What's in a name? For gardeners, plenty. Gardening is a blend of horticulture and botany, common names and high science, and the names can get a bit confusing. Whether you're looking at plant anatomy or simply want to know what to call a plant, understanding a bit about naming can help you wade through the aisles, ask better questions, and treat your plants right.

"Hello, my name is . . .": Getting used to plant nomenclature

Whenever you're talking about plants, knowing how they're named can help you avoid getting tangled up in the Latin. Generally, when looking for plants and flowers, you encounter two types of names — botanical and common. Read on for some info on how the naming system works, and then carpe diem — *pluck the day!*

Botanical names

The *botanical name* is the proper or scientific name of a plant. It consists of two parts: the genus name and the species name. The species name is kind of like your own first name (except it comes last in a plant's botanical name). The genus name is similar to your family name (except in botanical names, it comes first). For example, in the plant name *Hosta undulata,*

Hosta is the genus name, and *undulata* is the species name. *Hosta* describes an entire genus of famous, mostly shade-loving plants named hostas, and *undulata* describes the type of hosta it is — a hosta with an undulating leaf shape.

Sometimes the botanical name has a third name, right after the species name, known as the variety. A *variety* is a member of the same plant species but looks different enough to warrant its own name, such as *Rosa gallica var. officinalis.*

Still another botanical name that sometimes comes up is the *cultivar,* or cultivated variety. Cultivars are usually named by the people who developed or discovered them, and they're often maintained through cuttings, line-bred seed propagation, or tissue culture. In other words, they're cultivated (humans grow, improve, and develop them). An example is *Lychnis coronaria* 'Angel's Blush.'

Botanical names are more common with some types of plants than others. For instance, you frequently run into them with herbaceous plants, trees, and shrubs but much less so with roses, annuals, and vegetables. You can find botanical names on the labels and in many garden references.

Common names

Common names are what you're most likely to encounter when shopping for plants to put in your garden, and they're what you mostly encounter in this book. You can find these names prominently displayed on seed packets or on seedling trays of plants that are for sale. They're kind of like botanical nicknames that gardeners use to describe a certain type of plant without going into a great amount of detail. For example, the *Hosta undulata* fits into the genus

Hosta, so most gardeners merely refer to these plants under the common name of hostas. And you may know that *Hemerocallis* is actually the genus name for the common day lily, but chances are that most gardeners you encounter just call them day lilies.

Anatomy 101: Naming plant parts

Beyond recognizing the names of plants, knowing the various parts of plants is also useful. Figure 1-1 shows a nice, healthy perennial plant with the basic parts displayed. You probably already know most of them, but keep these parts in mind, because you need to know them to understand some of the things I discuss in the rest of this book! In the figure, the *taproot* is the main root of the plant; the *stolon,* or *runner,* is a horizontal stem that spreads through the ground to help some perennials propagate.

Sharing names with distant relatives

If you want to be absolutely sure of the plant you're buying, then remember that the botanical or scientific name, including the cultivar name, is the most exact one. Some common names, like *common basil,* are very specific. All common basil has the same genus and species, *Ocimum basilicum.* However, a common name like daisy is so general that it may not be very helpful. This term can apply to plants very faintly related found in various genera (genuses). For instance, a "daisy" can be an African daisy *(Arctotis* or *Gerbera),* Dahlberg daisy *(Dyssodia tenuiloba),* English daisy *(Bellis perennis),* painted daisy *(Chrysanthemum coccineum),* Shasta daisy *(Leucanthemum superbum),* and many others. If you're shopping by common names, read labels to make sure this particular kind of plant can grow for you.

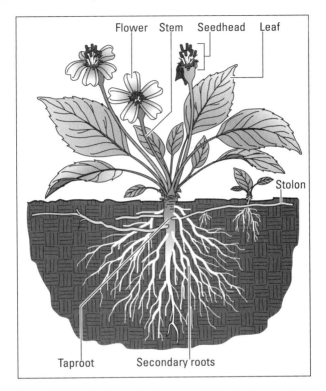

Figure 1-1: The basic parts of a perennial plant, above and below ground.

Bringing in Beauty with Flowers

Flowers are often the first thing that comes to mind when people think of gardening and the first thing people plan to grow when they want to beautify their surroundings. Flowers are marvelous because they come in a huge variety of sizes, colors, and shapes (see Figure 1-2), and no matter where you live, at least one kind of flowering plant can grow there. Even the volcanic crater of Haleakala, on the island of Maui, is home to a flowering plant: the rare silver sword.

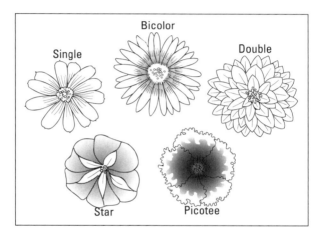

Figure 1-2: Flowers come in a wide variety of sizes and shapes, as these popular flowers show.

Flowers are more than merely the beautiful display they put on, however. If you know the different types of flowers out there, you can take full advantage of displaying them in your own garden.

Amazing annuals

You may already know what annuals are without realizing that you know! These beauties are the flowers, arrayed in flats and pots, for sale every spring down at the garden center — everything from geraniums to impatiens to marigolds. You bring them home and plunk 'em in the ground, and they get right to work, delivering pretty much continuous color all summer long. When fall comes, they start to slow down (some may even go to seed); cold weather eventually causes them to wither and die. Game over. (That is, unless you live in a frost-free climate; in this case, your "annuals" become perennials. See the upcoming section "Perennial plants" for more information.)

For the brief time annuals are growing and pumping out flowers, you get a lot of bang for your buck. A great deal of selection and breeding refinements over the years have made these plants totally reliable. They're hard to kill. Indeed, some of them keep blooming their cheery heads off even when you neglect them.

The rather unromantic term of *deadheading* simply refers to the practice of pinching or cutting off spent flowers. Your annuals look nicer when you do this, of course, but removing the flowers also serves another purpose: It thwarts the plant from the energy-intensive process of producing seeds, and the plant responds by diverting its energy back into making more flowers.

The main drawback of annuals is economic. You have to buy new ones every spring. If you're planting a wide area, running out to buy more year in and year out can get expensive. Time may also be an issue for you — you may grow sick and tired of getting down on your hands and knees and replanting.

You can use annuals

- ✔ To fill an entire flowerbed (this popular use is why some places call annuals *bedding plants*)

- ✔ In container displays — in pots, windowboxes, patio planter boxes, and more

- ✔ To fill a hanging basket

- ✔ To edge a walkway

- ✔ To "spot" color in a perennial bed

- ✔ In edging and as decoration for a vegetable or herb garden

- ✔ To cover over or at least distract from a fading spring bulb display

You can get an in-depth look at annuals in Chapter 5.

Perennial plants

For many gardeners, going from growing annuals to exploring perennials seems to be a natural progression. But remember that you don't have to choose! You can grow both and, indeed, your garden is likely to be the better for the diversity.

So, what exactly are *perennials?* They're long-lived herbaceous (non-woody) plants — flowers and herbs, mainly. How long they last depends on the plant and the conditions in your garden. But these plants certainly last longer than annuals.

A typical perennial emerges in the spring, grows and often produces flowers and seeds as the seasons progress from spring to summer to fall, and then slows down or dies back in winter. But the plant doesn't actually die; it just rests. The following spring, your perennial returns in glory to repeat the cycle.

Unlike annuals, you don't have to replant perennials every year. The life cycle of a perennial depends on various factors, notably the type of plant and whether it's happy in your garden. But you can certainly expect to get a minimum of two years and a maximum of a decade out of the vast majority of perennials. For best results, of course, take good care of them.

Annuals that aren't really annuals

False annuals are plants with tropical origins, or ones whose parents hail from the tropics, which means that they're actually perennial — more long-lived — somewhere, somewhere warmer, somewhere far away. These pseudo-annuals can, at least in theory, be kept going over the winter and live to dress up your garden again next year. Examples of these tropical visitors include the coleus, geranium, impatiens, salvia, snapdragon, and wax begonia.

Most perennials are slow starters. During their first year in your garden, they tend to invest in developing a good root system. Be patient! After that's established, they grow and expand, and the flower show gets better with each passing year.

Eventually, though, some perennials run out of steam. Their growth gets crowded and they don't seem to flower as well. At this time, you can dig them out and replace them, or you can divide them (perhaps discarding the tired-out center, or mother plant) and replant well-rooted bits for a fresh new start.

Here are some of the many uses of perennials:

- ✔ Creating a colorful bed or border
- ✔ Filling an *island bed* (an isolated, self-contained garden, like an "island" in a sea of lawn)
- ✔ Mixing them with annuals to assure summer-long color
- ✔ Edging a walkway, patio, pool area, or deck

> ✔ Interplanting them with roses or other ornamental shrubs to provide year-round interest
>
> ✔ Dressing up an area that was formerly lawn

Lots of places offer perennials these days. The garden centers in spring and early fall are full of them. Unless the place is especially big or sophisticated, you'll find mostly common, tried-and-true choices. If you get a taste for the more unusual perennials, or common ones in uncommon colors, turn to mail-order or Internet shopping. What's out there may astound you — thousands and thousands of fascinating and beautiful plants await!

For the details on perennials, check out Chapter 5.

Gardening for Your Dining Pleasure

For many gardeners, growing food is the real reason for gardening. There really isn't quite anything like the feeling of satisfaction a gardener gets from nurturing and encouraging a tomato plant to put forth the most gorgeous and delicious tomatoes imaginable.

Food-bearing plants come in all shapes, sizes, and types. Chapter 6 gives you the information you need to get started on growing your own vegetables.

Chapter 2

Planning Your Own Eden

. . . .

In This Chapter

▶ Working with what you already have

▶ Deciding on your garden style

▶ Staying within your budget

▶ Setting up your garden plans

. . . .

Consider your ideal garden. Perhaps you know you want a handsome woodland shade garden, but what'll it look like? Or maybe you know you want a sunny cottage garden, but what's your vision? Getting to this point in your garden planning is a bit like shopping for a blue shirt. You know you want a shirt and you know you want it to be blue, but you still have plenty of options. Now's the time to narrow in on your target.

By assessing your gardening wants, your gardening needs, and what you already have available for your garden, you can come up with the best garden for you. In this chapter, I lead you through the processes that can help you clarify your vision, and I explain how you can start making your dream garden a reality.

Taking Stock: Evaluating What You Already Have

Observation! That's the very first step. Forget for a moment what's growing in your neighbors' yards or other home landscapes around town that you see and may covet. It's time to take a broader view — it's all part of the assessing process, a process that can lead you to a gorgeous, successful garden of your own.

Here are the basic things to look for that affect your overall gardening plans. The following issues directly influence your planting decisions:

- ✔ **Local climate:** Over the course of a calendar year, is your area's climate dry or damp? Generally sunny or generally rainy? Do your winters (or summers) slow everything down or bring plant growth to a temporary halt? The answers to these questions can tell you which plants are likely to grow easily and which ones may require some extra help. See Chapter 3 for info about plant hardiness zones and how they affect your growing space.

- ✔ **Type of soil in your yard:** Consider the natural soil in your area. Is it rather sandy? Clay? Loamy (rich, crumbly, and dark)? Acidic? Alkaline? Does it drain rainwater away quickly, or does moisture puddle and linger for days? The answers can help you understand which plants will thrive and which ones will need soil improvements. (If you really don't have any idea, a simple soil test is a good idea — see Chapter 7.)

- ✔ **Plants native to your area (or already growing in your yard):** I'm not asking that you make a garden out of entirely native plants — after all, you may want to distinguish your yard from the surrounding natural landscape. But finding out which plants are native or perform well in your general area, either by observing or by asking around, can further fill you in on what kind of growing conditions you've been dealt.

And here are some structural considerations:

✔ **Permanence of big structures:** Okay, the house stays. The garage and shed, too, although maybe you can move or replace the shed. What about shade trees? Can and should you cut any of them down, or at least prune them? Big branches may be a hazard, and letting more light into a garden is often welcome.

✔ **Walkways:** It's hard, but not impossible, to change the path of foot traffic if it's currently in the way of your garden space. So take a hard look and be honest. If you add or replace a walking surface, the yard can look immediately nicer and your garden spot may be neatly outlined.

Options for installing a path include gravel, brick, flagstone, and other paving materials. Wandering paths look nicer and slow down footsteps, but pathways should actually lead somewhere if you want people to use them. Wider paths also slow people down and encourage them to enjoy their surroundings — your beautiful garden.

✔ **Desire for privacy or shelter:** Good fences can make good neighbors, and materials make all the difference. Big, substantial wooden fences do block street noise and unsightly views but may also create shade and look unfriendly. A lighter or more open design may be better, perhaps softened with a flowering, climbing plant.

An alternative is living fences of hedges or an informal line of bushes (evergreen or deciduous, with or without fruit and flowers). Work with what you have to improve your fence's look, or vow to install or replace it with something nicer.

Before making any major changes, consult with neighbors who'll be affected, especially if you have a neighborhood association that governs big yard projects.

Don't be intimidated by the beautifully designed and laid-out yards you see in your neighborhood or admire in the pages of gardening magazines or books. Transforming and beautifying your yard yourself, while bringing in outside help only if you think you need it, is perfectly possible. Like any other large project, you'll get further and feel better if you divide it into smaller parts.

Identifying problems and restrictions

There are certain classic gardening "problems" and, thankfully, myriad solutions. Please don't ever feel overwhelmed — picking out an area to work on and improve and concentrating your efforts can buoy your spirits, and then you can move on to another concern. My advice is to start first with an area you have the time and money to fix up — preferably an area you'd like to start enjoying sooner rather than later.

The main point is to take action. Address the big issues now, and you'll definitely feel well on your way to a more beautiful, enjoyable garden. Read on for some basic problems.

You have too much shade

A yard or garden space with a lot of shade is often lamented as forcing too many limitations on gardeners. This problem is often much easier to remedy than you may think, usually just by pruning trees and bushes:

1. **Go out with clippers and/or a small pruning saw to remove all "nonnegotiable" branches and twigs — anything obviously dead or diseased, particularly the lower branches of thick trees.**

2. **Go on to thinning — taking out growth that's rubbing against other branches or crowding the interior of a plant.**

3. **For anything you can't handle, call in a certified arborist or a tree company.**

    You need the services of a tree company if you decide to take out an entire tree. Check with local authorities; in some areas you need permission to cut down trees. In the end? More sun, more light, and more air — a whole new yard!

You have too much sun

If your garden space is sunnier than you'd like, the quick solution is to add human-made items — try an umbrella or two, a pergola (arbor), or an outdoor tent. For the long term, you can make a planting plan with shade trees and vines that cover trellises and other structures.

Your yard is too big

Here are three good ways to reduce that maintenance-demanding, water-hogging lawn and create ideal spaces for gardening:

✔ Create garden beds around the sides of the yard, widening or extending them as you can. Alternatively, create what landscapers call *island beds,* which are flat or mounded beds (in any shape and size you like) in the middle of a lawn.

✔ Add large, sprawling structures that take up a lot of yard space, such as pathways; a terrace, patio, or deck; a pool (swimming or ornamental); or a potting shed or gazebo. Adding garden beds around these structures really spruces things up.

✔ Fence in or otherwise enclose individual "garden rooms" within spaces around your yard. The fence can be an artificial fence made of wood or metal, or it can be made of hedges, ornamental grasses, or trellises overhung with vines.

Your yard is too little

A small yard can seem bigger, more welcoming, and a lot more charming when you employ a few basic gardening techniques. With these methods, you can transform your cozy little yard into the garden of your dreams:

✔ Soften the edges of your lawn so they don't seem so imposing. If you have a fence, you can paint the fence a bright color (dark colors heighten the sense of constriction), add lush vines or climbing roses, or adorn the fence with potted plants.

✔ Create a varied layering effect — that is, position different plant types and textures above and behind one another, stepping up to the edges of your yard. Some gardeners literally display a combination of in-ground and potted plants on and around a rack or stepladder.

✔ Add a focal point — a statue, a small fountain, or one spectacular pot or urn with a big, dramatic plant or showy combination of plants; this move draws attention away from the close boundaries.

The soil isn't the type or quality you want

More often than you may think, poor soil thwarts gardening plans. People just forget or underestimate the importance of having organically rich, well-draining ground to plant in.

To tackle this problem, try growing only those types of plants proven to work in your soil. See what the neighbors are growing in their gardens, or check with the local nursery for the best plants to grow in your area.

You can also dig into the soil and mix in the materials you want (sort of like making cake batter, only more work). A rototiller is a handy tool to use for this purpose. Remember to work down to a depth of 6 to 8 inches for most garden plants — less for shallow-rooted grass, more for trees and shrubs.

Too many weeds!

You can attack these unwelcome plants any time of the year, but you'll make faster progress if you start in late fall or early spring and thwart them before or just as they're sprouting. Use a hoe, smother weeds with plastic or mulch, or carefully use an herbicide (or some combination of these tactics). Then, in mid-summer, make sure you don't let weeds go to seed. Pull them, mow them down, and discard them outside your garden to keep them from coming back.

Taking advantage of your yard's assets

Every garden space has its strengths and its good spots, if only you look, and some of the "problems" I mention in earlier sections can actually be benefits if you see them that way. Here are a few examples of conditions you may find within your garden space and how to handle them:

- ✔ **Sunny days:** Bright sunshine is beloved by many plants, especially those with colorful flowers. Rejoice and be glad you have it; then go shopping for a wide range of bright and lively plants. Have fun with color combinations. Full sun also affords you the opportunity to grow many vegetables, herbs, fruits, and waterlilies.

- ✔ **The dark side:** If your lot in life is shade, don't fret. Consider it a gift, a chance to create a cool, soothing, even enchanting oasis. Without direct blasts from the hot sun, plants in a shady area look fresher and crisper for far longer. Wilting and withering in the heat aren't issues, colors don't get washed out, and not only do flowers last longer, but they also add sparkle and definition.

- ✔ **Dry conditions:** Instead of knocking yourself out trying to provide water for thirsty plants, seek out ones that prosper in drier growing conditions. A nursery that offers native plants (and good-looking cultivars of the same) is a good place to start. You don't have to grow only cacti and succulents, though you should check out the amazingly wide range of colors and shapes before you decide not to; lots of exciting dry-ground, drought-tolerant plants are available to gardeners.

✔ **Water:** If your yard's soggy or boggy, stop neglecting the area to weeds or trying to dry it out. Instead, grow plants that relish damp ground. Loads of good-looking choices — large and small, tall and ground-covering, flowering and foliage — are available. Try red twig dogwood, red maples, skunk cabbage, or Japanese primroses.

Getting Ideas for Your Garden Space

After you take inventory of your garden space and yard in general, consider what *sort* of garden you want. Before you get bogged down in choosing plants and deciding where to plant them, think in broad terms once again. How do you want to use your garden? What are your needs and expectations? Naming your goals can help you further clarify the details of your plans.

If I had one single, strong piece of advice to give you at this point — and I do! — it would be this: Be realistic. Identify, admit, and allow for special uses and considerations. Working within an honest, clear-eyed framework is so much easier. A beautiful garden can grow up around your "givens."

Gardening with the kids in mind

If you have young children of your own, or if kids are always visiting, plan for them and their antics. A flower border of precious perennials, some of them delicately supported by stakes, will be in constant danger of being trampled if kids ride bikes or play rousing games of soccer nearby. Although placing your raised-bed vegetable garden right in the center of a sunny lawn may be logical, figure out whether the kids' fun and games can work around it or whether the kids will be running through it.

As parents everywhere know, the key to lowering your frustration level is being flexible. Site the perennials way at the back of the lawn area if you must; shield flowers with a fence or picnic table or living barrier, such as a line of shrubs or berry bushes; locate that vegetable garden more off to the side; and so on. You get the idea.

With kids' short attention spans and wish for quick gratification, it's unlikely that you'll be able to get the children to help you dig up a new planting area, nor would it be safe or advisable to have them help with pruning projects. But you have plenty of other ways to build your kids' interest in gardening:

✔ **Raise some easy-to-grow plants for kids.** Favorites include green beans (pole beans, on a teepee, so kids can have a fort inside), nasturtiums, morning glories, mini pumpkins, and sunflowers.

✔ **Plant things kids love to harvest, whether vegetables or flowers for bouquets.** Just make sure you supervise children, especially if they're using clippers or scissors.

✔ **Encourage help by putting money in the till.** Don't forget the time-honored tradition of paying your budding entrepreneurs for pulling weeds — though the going rate is probably no longer a penny a dandelion!

Creating space for entertainment

A popular trend these days is outdoor rooms or outdoor living, and it's easy to see why. When good weather comes, who can resist hanging out or dining in the fresh air?

Patio gardens, decks, and terraces adjacent to the house (front, side, or back) continue to be popular because you and your guests have easy access to the house. People can easily pop inside for additional food, drink, or supplies; to use the restroom; or to dispose of trash. Screened-in spots may be necessary if you have a mosquito or other bug problem and still want to be comfortable outside.

We've witnessed a recent boom in outdoor furniture options — styles as well as materials. From rust-resistant tables, chairs, and benches, to mildew-resistant cushions in bright colors, to handsome but practical umbrellas, you can have a set that looks great even when left out in the sun and rain. Just feast your eyes on the choices at your local home-supply store, big-box retail store, or mail-order gardening supplier. The outdoor lifestyle has never offered so many excellent and attractive choices. Choose stuff that meets your needs, is durable, and has style and color that match or enhance or set the tone for the surrounding garden. (You may also invest in attractive, fitted covers for everything to protect items from the elements when not in use.)

Outdoor entertainment areas ought to connect to the garden so that although people are enjoying indoor-style comforts and amenities, people are still able to savor the unique joys of being outside. You can incorporate potted plants (both colorful flowers and practical herbs or veggies), set out vases of flowers cut from the garden, add hanging baskets, and plant right up to the perimeters. To create a transition from the outdoor entertainment area and the garden proper (and thus gracefully blend them), repeat elements in both places — use the same or similar plants, or incorporate the same or complementary colors.

Add flair and beauty to your outdoor entertaining area with wind chimes, candles, citronella torches, lanterns, or windsocks.

 Whatever you decide to set up, remember to imagine and then accommodate foot traffic — people will wear a path anyway, so plan for it.

Designing a sanctuary: The quiet garden retreat

A garden retreat needs to be outside and away from the busy world, where you can relax and gather your thoughts in peace, quiet, and solitude. Having a simple and undemanding landscaping and décor can encourage you to relax, not jump up to attend to garden chores or errant weeds.

You needn't turn your entire garden to a Zen-like space. A special corner or tucked-away nook will do. Privacy, protection, and isolation are key elements of a good retreat. Think about adding a fence or wall to block out sights and, equally importantly, sounds. Less-solid screens in the shape of trellises or tall and dense plantings of trees and shrubs or even a gathering of potted plants can also enclose a space. The idea is to make a garden room accessible yet insulated. For summertime relaxation, consider a shady retreat.

Within the walls of your retreat, make a comfortable place to sit or even recline. A full table-and-chairs set is appropriate if you plan to share the space and enjoy meals or quiet cups of tea here. A hammock or a chaise lounge invites reading and relaxing.

Now consider the furnishings — namely, plants and décor:

- ✔ The plants that you choose should be easygoing selections that don't require fussing — for shade, try impatiens; for sun, marigolds or zinnias are good choices. Stick to a simple or even monochromatic color scheme, one that's soothing to the eye.

- ✔ Consider a water element, such as a small, tubbed water garden or fountain. The inherently soothing sight and sound of water can help block out distracting noises.

- ✔ A judiciously employed ornament, such as a hummingbird feeder, a large clay urn, a garden statue of St. Fiacre (the patron saint of gardeners), or Buddha, can further the mood.

Cooking up an edible garden: Gardening for your kitchen

If you love to cook and enjoy gardening, it's only a matter of time before you long to grow your own produce. A so-called kitchen garden can be modest in size, easy to manage, and produce all the fresh vegetables and herbs you desire.

Because a kitchen garden exists for one reason — to generate good things to eat — planting it near your house is best. That way, you can pop out the door, snip the herbs you need or grab a few sun-warmed cherry tomatoes, and put them to immediate use.

Ideally, a kitchen or dining-room window overlooks your patch so you aren't likely to forget what's ripe for the taking.

If your goal is to serve healthier and fresher food to your family, go for a variety of classic vegetables and herbs. Even salad skeptics may be won over after they taste a wondrous array of colorful lettuces accompanied by fresh ripe tomatoes. And kids who don't normally enjoy vegetables can discover the joys of fresh, sweet homegrown peas and carrots. (For more on raising vegetables, consult Chapter 6.)

The easiest, most successful kitchen gardens are small and simple. You can always expand later. To get started, I recommend

- **Keeping it sunny:** At least six hours of full sun per day is essential for good growth and ripening of almost all vegetables, herbs, and edible flowers. Morning light is preferable to afternoon because it dries the dew (reducing the risk of disease) and is less stressful than the blazing heat of midafternoon.

- **Setting the boundaries:** Stake out a spot using string rigged between wooden sticks, or try a simpler approach: Use your garden hose as a guide. After you establish the garden, you can edge the bed with bricks or stones or commercial plastic edging. Or dig a roughly 4-inch-deep trench all around the edges. The idea is to keep any lawn grass from encroaching on your kitchen garden.

- **Building raised beds:** If the soil in the appointed spot isn't very good, erect a raised bed from planks standing on edge. Be sure to use untreated lumber, because some wood preservatives may be harmful to edible plants. (Unless you use the more expensive cedar, these wooden sides will eventually rot and need replacing. By then, you may be ready to expand your kitchen garden, anyway.)

✔ **Installing protective barriers:** If you garden in deer, woodchuck, or rabbit territory (just to name some of the worst pests), or if you host backyard soccer games, a protective fence around your kitchen garden may be in order. Use poultry wire or wood and sink it into the ground to discourage digging invaders. If the fence doesn't look very attractive, plant fast-growing, lightweight plants to cover it, such as morning glories.

✔ **Planting a few containers that are literally at the kitchen door:** Try a small tomato plant surrounded by 'Spicy Globe' basil, a cut-and-come-again mix of lettuces and salad greens, and another container of your favorite herbs.

Zeroing In on Your Ideal Garden Style

After you've determined your basic wants and needs for your garden space, you're ready to decide on its overall style. Gardens come in many types, themes, and moods. Yours can be informal, with less strict boundaries, a more casual look, and a wide variety of plants; or it can be formal, with symmetrical lines, crisp edges, and a limited plant palette. Or it can be one of many variations in between.

Select a style based on the architecture of your house, the lay of the land, or even an idea you saw in a magazine. Your choice also ought to take into consideration the advantages and disadvantages already inherent in your yard and gardening space, as I outline earlier in this chapter.

A garden is an emotional place for many people — a place of pride and joy, of relaxation, comfort, and meaningful projects. Luckily, a garden's always a work in progress, and you can improve, expand, or totally change some or all of it over time. You should also be open to surprises, like the errant sunflower that pops up near the deck or the herb that self-sows into the roses and ends up looking pretty there. So dream and plan, but be flexible.

Gardening around a theme

Garden design often goes beyond the types of plants you want to grow and the type of function you want your garden to have. Thematic elements can also influence the look of a garden. Do you have a soft spot for old-fashioned English rose gardens? Or Japanese Zen gardens? Or even sandy deserts filled with cacti and succulents? In the following sections, I list some popular style elements to help you continue clarifying what you may want and need.

If you'd like your garden to be like the styles covered in this book or any other of the large variety of garden styles available, be sure to do plenty of research beforehand to make your space look as harmonious and authentic as possible. And don't forget to make sure your space can accommodate the style! Trying to install an outdoor cactus garden in the Midwest USA may not be your best bet.

Formal gardens

Keep formal gardens simple (see Figure 2-1; common names are presented for plants you might want to consider using). Aim for balance and symmetry so the garden has an air of calm elegance. Here are some tips:

✔ Use strong lines and boundaries, such as groomed hedges, walkways, perhaps even a reflecting pool.

✔ Employ single-color plantings, aiming to match or complement your house color, fence, or another element.

✔ Add stylish pots, urns, gazing balls, or statuary. Keep everything in moderation so it doesn't look cluttered.

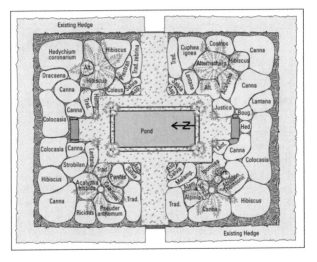

Figure 2-1: A complete garden plan for a classy, formal garden.

Asian gardens

Asian gardens (Figure 2-2) are usually based on a *garden floor,* or a broad area of raked sand or stones. Choose fine-textured traditional plants, in pots or in the ground. Try bamboo, dwarf conifers, Japanese maples, iris, azalea, and flowering fruit trees. Then include Oriental-style accessories such as stone lanterns, bamboo fencing, a water basin, or even a small "tea house."

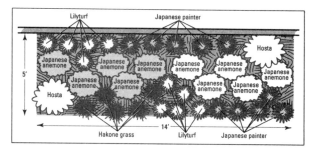

Figure 2-2: A garden plan featuring an Asian-inspired design.

Tropical gardens

Put a piece of paradise in your own backyard. Tropical gardens (Figure 2-3) emphasize lots of big, bold, leafy foliage plants (such as cannas, coleus, hibiscus, and taro) in the ground or in large containers. Use bright flowers in hot colors: yellow, red, and orange, as well as bicolors. Then include a water feature, such as a pool, fountain, or stream. You can add drama with extras: birdhouses or cages, colorful pots, gazing balls, and playful or handcrafted décor and statuary.

Cottage gardens

Cottage gardens should be overflowing with colorful blooms, so plant these inviting, informal gardens with a generous hand. Include lots of roses and other fragrant plants (including herbs). Keep the plants

well-tended (remove spent flowers and stems) but
allow them to express their natural exuberance.
Finally, add some charming touches — a picket fence,
an arbor, whimsical birdhouses, or wind chimes.

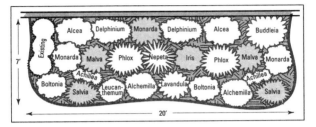

Figure 2-3: A garden plan featuring a planting with a tropical
feel.

Dry climate gardens

If your area is a little on the parched side, you may
want to opt for a dry climate garden. Employ a natu-
ralistic layout, perhaps with a dry streambed or stone
pathways, and choose plants that thrive in hot sun,
including but not limited to cacti and succulents.
Then strategically place accents of colorful or more
water-needy plants in pots or in groups.

Woodland gardens

Woodland gardens, which are often shady, include
groundcovers that flower as well as bulbs (for lots of
spring color). For fall color, you can plant some
native asters.

This garden is most practical if you already have a
well-treed lot. Tall deciduous hardwoods like oaks,
beeches, and maples are ideal because they provide
a high canopy with diffused shade. Seek out diverse

forms and colors for the larger plants, from bold hostas to lacy ferns. You can then tuck in non-plant items for color and interest, such as ornaments and garden furniture.

An inspired idea: Perusing books, magazines, and local gardens

As part of your narrowing-down process, have fun as you gather inspiration. Thumb through back issues of gardening magazines, flagging beautiful photographs and helpful articles. Grab a few of those arguably fluffy gardening magazines you often see at the check-out stand at the grocery store.

Also check the gardening books you already own, both practical ones and coffee-table books, and do the same. Visit a well-stocked bookstore or the book section at a garden center and do some more prospecting. Buy a few titles if you find something wonderful and useful.

And don't forget the gardens that aren't too far beyond your front door. Bring your camera as you visit your local botanical garden or arboretum, and take advantage of local garden tours. Walk around surrounding neighborhoods and take pictures of gardens or vignettes that pique your interest.

The object of this exercise is to fill your mind with enticing images of what's possible. You also get to see how other gardeners — in various regions, with different types of yards — have pulled off their woodland garden or cottage garden or whatever you're aiming for. Study their creativity and their solutions; they can help you clarify your vision.

Tackling the paste-and-ponder method

Some people find their ideas jell best given a little time. If you have an available wall or large bulletin board, try this: Rip out inspirational photos from magazines, gather your photos, and tack them up. Make the display orderly or make it a collage. Then leave it there and walk by every now and then, pausing to admire and study it. Add to it, shift things around, and take pieces away.

This admittedly informal method can really help clarify your thinking and consolidate your planning, especially if you're a visually oriented person. The paste-and-ponder method also helps you keep your eye on the prize, so leave the board up for a while.

Making Sure Costs Don't Outgrow Your Budget

Having a good garden, or a series of smaller gardens on your property, does cost money. Fencing materials and paving stones aren't cheap. Garden furnishings and décor aren't cheap. Big plants, special small plants, and pots aren't cheap. Potting soil and loam aren't cheap. Fertilizer and pesticides aren't cheap. It all adds up. And, frankly, budgeting is hard when you're dealing with an ongoing project whose look is likely to evolve.

So here's my main advice: Relax. Rome wasn't built in a day. Take small bites, if need be. Tackle one project at a time and see it through, and then move on to the next one. Or divide a large project into sections and allow yourself time — even several seasons or years — to complete it.

One place where you can save money is labor — use yourself, involve your partner or your kids, bribe friends with dinner, or hire neighborhood kids. And remember that, fortunately, gardening is one of those experiences in life whose journey can be as satisfying as the destination.

 Here are some other money-saving ideas:

- ✔ Grow plants from seed.

- ✔ Divide perennials and shrubs and move the pieces to other parts of your yard.

- ✔ Get plants from other gardeners — some people may simply give you their unwanted surplus; others will be happy to swap. Join a local garden club, and you may be assured of these transactions!

- ✔ Make your own compost. And always compost your fall leaves instead of bagging them and sending them off to the local landfill.

- ✔ Buy from the source, whether it's a special day lily nursery nearby or a local brickyard.

- ✔ Browse yard sales, junkyards, and antique shops. You may happen across real bargains in garden ornaments as well as pots, gates, trellises, fencing, and so on.

Last but not least, take care of your investments. It's a sad waste to let good, costly plants or garden areas languish or die. The more you know about soil, about planting, about plant care — and this book is chock-full of useful advice — the easier it'll be to do right by your garden. A thriving garden can repay you many times over.

Bringing Your Garden Ideas to Reality

Armed with your ideas and goals and wishes, step outside and bring your plans to life. Some gardeners find that the best time to do this step is fall or winter, when you have fewer distractions from overgrown plants and seasonal clutter. The outline and the "bones" of a yard are more evident then. But whenever you do this step, look beyond what's present. Visualize what will change and what will go in.

When you're ready to sketch out your garden plan, you can do it yourself or, if it seems daunting or is simply not your cup of tea, you can hire a licensed professional. Your overall garden plan doesn't have to be precise or perfect. It just has to do what you need it to do — show you your yard so you can plan what you want to put into it.

Sketching out the yard you have now

Using graph paper and the tools necessary to draft out your garden (see Figure 2-4), draw a plan of your site to scale, say ¼" for each foot. Plot every feature you find on your site, both natural and those you or your predecessors have put in place. Use a measuring tape to get at least approximate measurements. You may want to indicate areas of sun and shade.

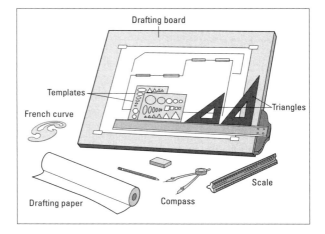

Figure 2-4: There are many ways to draft out your garden plan, but here are the tools you need to get started.

If you'd like, you can also use photography to help sketch out your plans, Photograph panoramic sequences of every part of your property, as well as external features (such as views) you may want to enhance or hide. Paste them together to form a wide-angle shot.

Making your drawing match your dream garden

After you've completed the initial drawing of your yard or garden plot, you can add the elements for your garden plan. Here are some recommendations:

1. **Gather any pictures you're using for inspiration, and prepare a list of your main goals, assets, and limitations.**

Go to the earlier section "Taking Stock: Evaluating What You Already Have" for advice on looking at your yard's challenges and advantages. "Getting Ideas for Your Garden Space" can help you focus on your gardening goals.

2. **Study your current plan carefully.**

   Decide which features you want to incorporate into your final plan, which ones you want to highlight, and which ones you want to downplay or remove.

3. **Place a piece of tracing paper over your plan.**

4. **Use a pencil and sketch in or leave out various features and designs.**

   Try hard to stick to your theme or overall vision, and attempt to be organized (see "Zeroing In on Your Ideal Garden Style" for details on themes).

 When designing your garden plan, you don't have to get bogged down in details, listing every plant by name. Instead, "sun-loving perennials," "blue and yellow bed," or "pots of annuals" may suffice.

After all the elements you've planned for are in place, take a good look at them to make sure the overall drawing matches the initial image of the dream garden you had in your head. If something looks awkward or looks like it needs to be moved or changed in any way, do so! Keep changing that drawing (and redrawing it if necessary) until you have a final plan that satisfies you.

Defining key areas so you know where to start

With your sketched yard in hand, your next step is to decide which area you want to start with and to roll up your sleeves. As I repeatedly advise, tackling everything at once isn't easy and often isn't realistic or affordable. Break big projects down into manageable pieces, and do them one at a time.

Like rooms in a house, a garden area has four major elements. And as in building a house, going from the ground up is best. Tackle the four major elements in this order:

1. **Floor:** Lawn grass, a groundcover, paving materials, or good, plantable soil

2. **Walls:** Supplied literally by a wall of your house; by a fence, hedge, or trellis; or by a backdrop of evergreens or shrubs of some kind

3. **Ceiling:** Can certainly be open sky but may also involve an umbrella, awnings, overarching tree or large-shrub branches, or a pergola with or without a cloak of plants

4. **Furniture:** Literally tables and chairs and benches and the like, but also major containers or garden ornaments and décor

Don't go overboard with garden gnomes and pink flamingos. Limit yourself to one or two ornaments and keep the focus on the sense of space and the living parts of your garden.

Chapter 3

Getting into the Zone — Your Garden's Zone

....

In This Chapter

▶ Deciphering hardiness zones

▶ Growing in seasonal frost zones

....

*N*ewcomers to gardening are often baffled by all the talk of zones in gardening magazines, books, catalogs, and plant labels. You may sense that this zone business is some kind of secret code or language that's hard to remember or tricky to understand. It's not. It's really a simple (if generalized) system for describing climate so you can figure out whether a plant ought to be able to grow where you live.

This chapter helps you know and navigate the zones so you can put the information to use and pick out the right plants as you plan or add to your garden.

Different Hardiness Zone Maps for Different Folks

If all that gardeners ever grew were locally adapted plants, you'd have no reason to find out or concern yourself with hardiness zones. But of course, you want it all, right? You want to grow exotic goodies from distant lands or plants from allegedly similar but far-off places. So after your initial infatuation with a plant that's new to you, you can ask yourself, "Is growing this in my garden possible?" Finding out the plant's appropriate zone gives you an answer.

Just to complicate matters, different zone maps are out there, and some are better depending on where you live. The USDA Plant Hardiness Zone Map is the most prevalent one that gardeners in North America use, but others exist. The American Horticultural Society's Heat-Zone Map is more useful and popular for people in the Southern and Western USA, while Sunset's Garden Climate Zones Map, though complex, serves the Western states well.

 Despite all the zone maps and all the research, hardiness remains an inexact science. Although some plants turn out to be surprisingly tough, others succumb unexpectedly. The easiest thing you can do is to set your sights on plants said to be appropriate for your area. Here are some tips on deciding what you can grow, even if you're not sure about the zone:

✔ **Peek at your neighbors' yards.** Chances are that if a type of plant is succeeding right nearby, it can grow well, survive, and thrive for you, too.

✔ **Buy local.** When you get plants that were raised in your area (not in some distant place or coddled in a greenhouse), they're much more likely to be able to handle whatever your local weather dishes out.

✔ **Grow native plants.** Plants that come from your area or region — ones you've seen growing in the wild, perhaps, or certainly in local parks or botanic gardens — are sure to be well-adapted and set not only to survive but to prosper. How do you know whether a plant is native? Ask where you buy, or look it up.

Taking a look at plant hardiness zone maps

Every part of the world has its own hardiness zones, and most maps are set up the same way. The USDA Plant Hardiness Zone Map, for example, is a color-coded or shaded map, sometimes accompanied by a chart that expresses the same information. You can see the map (and others) in many places after you become tuned in to it — a poster tacked up on the wall at your local garden center, the back flyleaf of gardening books, in the back pages of most garden magazines, or tucked into the interior of your favorite gardening catalog. You can also access it online at www.usna.usda.gov/Hardzone/ushzmap.html.

The United States Department of Agriculture published, and has occasionally modified and updated, this hardiness zone map of North America. The most recent map, based on climate data gathered at National Weather Service stations throughout the U.S. and by weather stations throughout Canada and Mexico, came out in 1990. You can find 11 zones marking the average lowest winter temperatures, with Zones 2–10 divided into subzones.

Canada's plant hardiness zone map shows nine zones, based on average climatic conditions and altitude of each area. The harshest zone is 0, and the mildest is 8. In addition, the major zones are further divided into subzones. For example, Zone 4 splits into 4a and 4b, where zone *a* is slightly colder than zone *b*. You can see Canada's map at `atlas.nrcan.gc.ca/ site/english/maps/environment/land/ planthardi`.

Warming up to the heat-zone map

The USDA map, although enormously popular and widely used, has its limitations. For example, Zone 7 in Maryland is a world away from Zone 7 in Oregon, or north Texas, or the foothills of California's Sierra Nevada mountains. In many parts of the country, heat rather than cold dictates which plants are able to survive from one year to the next.

Thus, in 1997 (after years of study and research), the American Horticultural Society released its own map, the AHS Heat-Zone Map. Though still relatively new and still being tweaked, this map has proven quite useful to gardeners in the South and West. You can download the Heat-Zone Map at `www.ahs.org/ publications/heat_zone_map.htm`.

The AHS map has 12 zones. Relatively cooler Zone 1 is defined as having only one day of 86°F weather per year; sweltering Zone 12 has 210 days of such heat or more. (Research has shown that 86°F is the temperature at which many plants — that is, their cells, or plant tissue — start to experience damage from heat. That's why that point became the baseline for laying out the heat zones.)

U.S. gardeners in areas where the main source of plant stress is not winter cold but summer heat prefer this system. If the heat-zone information isn't supplied for a plant you're interested in, look in newer regional reference books and plant catalogs and Web sites.

Savoring the Sunset zones

In the Western USA — a region loosely defined as the states of Arizona, Utah, New Mexico, California, Nevada, Idaho, Montana, Wyoming, Colorado, Oregon, and Washington — neither the USDA Zone Map nor the AHS Zone Map gives complete enough information. Complex and varied terrain and dramatic weather variations conspire to make this particular region unique.

So the Sunset Publishing Company, based in the San Francisco area, devised its own Garden Climate Zone Map, which you can find online at www.sunset.com/garden/climate-zones. You may also see it in many publications, from books to subscriber-driven magazines to newsstand issues. Gardeners, landscapers, and nurseries in the West often refer to these Sunset zones.

Sunset's zone map contains 45 zones. Yep, 45. These zones actually cover the entire U.S., Southern Canada, and Northern Mexico, and they're all very individualized and specific. For example, Sunset Zone 3 is defined as *West's Mildest High-elevation and Interior Regions* and covers much of the area east of the Cascades in the Northwest, where residents see snow cover in winters but also blazing summers. Zone 16 is *Northern and Central California Coast Range Thermal Belts,* from Santa Barbara County to Marin County; this area gets drying summer winds, fog, and a climate made mild by proximity to the ocean.

These Sunset zones can particularly empower a new or frustrated Western USA gardener, especially if the source of plants also uses the same zones. So ask at the local nursery or garden center, or go out and buy

Sunset publications tailored to your particular zone and do some reading and research; then go shopping near or far when you know just what you want.

Reading plant hardiness zone maps

Take a look at the USDA Plant Hardiness Zone Map at `www.usna.usda.gov/Hardzone/ushzmap.html`. Notice that Zone 1, at the top or northernmost part of the map, is coldest; Zone 11 is at the bottom, or southernmost part, and is warmest. In terms of hardiness zones established in the USA, Zones 1 and 11 represent the extremes. The bulk of the United States, though, fits into Zones 5, 6, 7, and 8. Originally, the zones were conceived to be 10°F apart.

As you study the map, say you find that you live in USDA Zone 7. So you determine that this means

✔ You should be able to grow any tree, shrub, or perennial labeled "hardy to USDA Zone 7."

✔ You probably can't grow plants that are less cold-hardy, such as Zone 8 or 9 ones — your colder winters may harm or kill them.

✔ You can grow plants labeled for farther north, even more cold-tolerant ones said to be "hardy to Zone 6 or 5."

However, every rule has an exception. Most gardeners can stray one, maybe two USDA zones from their own when making plant choices and the gamble will pay off.

You often see a plant's projected USDA Hardiness Zones expressed as a range. For instance, most clematis hybrids are said to be "hardy in Zones 3 to 8." This statement means anyone gardening in Zones 3, 4, 5, 6, 7, or 8 ought to be able to grow one; the plant should survive your winters.

Basic zones are based on the average annual minimum temperature — in other words, as cold as winter gets. Thus, in the USDA Plant Hardiness Zone Map, Zone 6's lowest winter temperature (on average) is –10°F.

Why base zone maps on cold temperatures? After all, other things doom plants, such as high heat, lack of water, too much water, too much or too little sun, and the wrong soil. But over centuries, people found that cold is a better predictor of what will survive than any of those other (admittedly important) factors.

Fathoming Frost Zones and Growing Seasons

Whether a plant can survive the winter isn't your only concern. You know annuals are going to live for only one season, but you also want to know how long that season will be. After all, you may not be pleased if your dahlias die before flowering or your tomato plants freeze before producing much fruit. Unfortunately, hardiness zones don't tell you much about the length of the growing season. Enter the frost zone map.

Zones are determined not only by temperatures but also by the *climate,* which combines temperature readings, rainfall, humidity, wind, air pressure, and other factors. Climates in frost zone maps are generally determined by *growing season,* the time during which — hold onto your hats — plants add new growth. The last spring frost and the first fall frost bookend the growing season, marking a nice period of frost-free days. Basically, this time period is your window of opportunity to plant, nurture, and enjoy your home landscape.

The length of a growing season varies somewhat from year to year but is generally about the same. You probably already have a sense of your growing season, but if you really need to know, finding out is fairly easy. Call your nearest Cooperative Extension Service office, ask a knowledgeable gardener or garden-center staffer, or watch your local newspaper for the frost dates (which can vary from one year to the next). Many gardeners also use frost zone maps, like the one here: www.avant-gardening.com/zone.

Here's how to calculate your growing season: Suppose you live in Denver, Colorado; your last frost is May 3, and your first fall freeze is October 8. That gives you 157 days in which to garden.

Winter doesn't mean a gardener can or should be idle in the downtime. You can find plenty to do if you're so inclined to capitalize on the "shoulder seasons." You can be plotting for the future, starting seeds indoors with the plan to put them out in the ground the minute the last spring frost passes; you can be reading more about plants; you can be fussing with cleaning and sharpening your tools; you can enjoy your-self as you care for indoor plants; and you can be placing orders with mail-order suppliers — all activities that feed into the process and joy of having a wonderful garden.

Chapter 4

Gathering Your Gardening Gear

You can find deep and abiding pleasure in a good tool, in finding and using the right equipment for the job at hand. This statement is as true for gardening as it is for, say, cooking or woodworking. In this chapter, I survey some tools you probably need (and want) to aid you with your gardening, and I advise you on their selection and care.

The difference between the right tool and the wrong tool is the difference between back-breaking labor and joyful efficiency.

Digging Those, Er, Digging Tools

Dogs (and kids) often dig for no apparent reason, for the sheer pleasure of getting deeper into the ground and letting the dirt fly. Gardeners, on the other hand, dig with a purpose — to create a new planting bed or hole, to create a trench, or to harvest a delicious, home-grown root vegetable. Nonetheless, gardeners have the right to have fun in the dirt! And having fun turning the soil is possible when you have the right tool.

Getting down with shovels and spades

Shovels and spades are digging tools, and you may be astounded at the array available. However, generally speaking, digging tools fall into two main types: shovels and spades. Choosing one within a type requires matching it to your needs — the sort of soil it'll be digging, plus your own height and body strength.

 What's the difference between a shovel and a spade? Well, generally, it comes down to the shape of the digging edges:

- ✔ **Shovels have rounded edges.** The rounded tip is meant to allow easy, sword-like penetration of a variety of soils and materials. You also want a dish that's stiff and strong and able to hold dirt.

- ✔ **Spades have square edges.** The purpose of this digging tool is to lift, move, and throw with ease. It's supposed to be easier on your back — just slightly flex your knees and thrust it in and out of the pile of leaves, compost, or topsoil you're working on.

When you go shovel (or spade) shopping, you may observe various grades and prices. You get what you pay for, folks. A so-called "homeowner" or "economy" shovel looks good enough, but it may not stand up to tougher jobs or rocks in the ground. Contractor shovels, on the other hand, have a thicker blade and strong attachments for forging where the blade meets the handle. Be sure to pay close attention to the labels to know what kind of shovel you're looking at. You can usually find a range of quality at a single store.

Forged shovels and spades are the best because they're made of a single piece of metal. Stamped ones are okay for lighter jobs, but because the metal is cut from a single thickness, they're not as strong or tailored to a job.

 To determine whether a shovel is well-made, examine where parts come together (assuming the shovel you're contemplating is not all one piece). Rivets and welding points are weak spots, though often necessary. Avoid anything with sloppy workmanship. The following sections outline other things to look for.

A strong shaft

The reason the shaft is straight is simple: Bends or curves create weak or stress points. Do check that the tool you're thinking of buying has a nice, straight handle. Material is equally important. A "solid hardwood handle," although desirable, is also rather vague. You want a strong, solid, splinter-resistant wood; ash is considered the best, with hickory in second place. Maple is okay, too, though it's heavier and can break in unpredictable ways.

 Painted shafts? No doubt they're attractive in their jaunty color and smooth texture, but beware: A coat of paint may be hiding weaknesses or flaws, such as knots or grafted pieces of wood. Better to go with a plain, unadorned model so you can see what you're getting (and paint it yourself at home if you'd like).

Metal (including steel) and fiberglass handles are also available. Though they can be quite strong and weather-tough, their drawback is that when they bend or break, the tool is finished. And either of these materials may transport uncomfortable or numbing vibrations into your hands and arms. Also, metal tools can be darn cold during the winter (and they conduct electricity — yikes!).

The correct handle

You need good leverage; the right grip, well-designed and durably constructed, delivers just that. Seek a comfortable fit for your hand and peer closely at the rivets that attach the handle to be sure they're neatly installed and flush. You'll likely see the classic D-handle most often, usually made of durable but lightweight plastic (which can and does crack or break down over the years due to use and exposure to sunlight, though you can certainly get many good years out of it). A good handle is easy and comfortable to hang onto, especially during twisting and lifting motions.

A variation on the D-handle is the so-called YD handle, which is longer and potentially sturdier. The two sides of the handle converge in a Y, and a crosspiece of wood (usually metal-reinforced) joins them. This design has the advantage of dissipating twisting forces.

The T-handle is excellent for two-handed pushing work, such as in the shallow-angled spades that gardeners use to edge planting beds or peel off turf or topsoil. The drawback is that the impact of your digging travels straight into your wrist, so look for a coated handle or wear gloves to alleviate the shock, at least somewhat.

A good angle or cant

Cant refers to the angle between the head of the spade or shovel and the ground. A lower angle is best for digging and holding soil; a steeper angle is better suited to lifting and tossing soil and other materials. To check the cant, place the tool on the ground and see how flat it lies.

A well-designed frog

The *frog* is the open-backed tube or socket, meant to fit the head of the tool to the shaft. It's vulnerable to collecting dirt along its length, so unless you assiduously clean your shovel after every use, the dirt eventually starts to rot the wooden handle. Some shovels have metal welded over this area to prevent that, although the front side is still a point of weakness.

Trowels: More than just little shovels

A good trowel is an indispensable gardening friend, with you for many years. Consider everything I say here, but definitely pick one that feels right to you when you hold and use it. As with shovels and spades, many different kinds of trowels are on the market. You have plenty of choices, so be sure to pay attention to the labels at the store and ask for assistance if you have trouble determining which trowel is right for you.

Good-quality materials make for a more effective, longer-lasting trowel. The blade (from cheapest on up to best) is made from

- ✔ Stamped metal
- ✔ Aluminum
- ✔ Forged carbon steel or (no rust!) stainless steel

Top-of-the-line trowels feature a carbon steel blade that's epoxy-coated to resist wear and rust. As for the handle, good, strong wood is what you want — ash or hickory is best. Avoid cheap trowels of lightweight materials, because they seem to bend or even break at the slightest challenge.

A sign of a quality trowel, one that can stand lots of use, is one whose wooden handle meets its metal blade in a strong and lasting manner so it won't bend or break.

 One-piece metal trowels may send tiring shock-waves into your hands as you work and be icy cold to the touch, but manufacturers have solved this problem by coating the handle with rubber or PVC plastic. For other types, seek a smooth wooden handle so you don't get splinters or blisters. In any event, you should be able to squeeze the handle comfortably, with little stress to your wrist.

Some trowels have a hole drilled into the very top part of the handle, perhaps with a string or leather thong loop for hanging and storing the tool when it's not in use. Though this feature may seem frivolous, it can be a handy extra if you're the sort of person who needs to be reminded to bring your gardening tools indoors and clean them up after use. Another feature you may appreciate is a ruler stamped or etched into the blade — built-in rulers are helpful when you're planting bulbs or other flowers that require varying planting depths.

Garden forks: Not for dining!

Although not an essential garden tool, many garden-ers come to find that a garden fork is quite handy and more agile than a spade or shovel for some digging jobs. You drive this shovel-size tool into the soil and then pull back on the handle and rock it to break and loosen soil. It's useful for digging up bulbs and root crops, including onions and potatoes. It's also good for scooping jobs (moving compost from one spot to another, for instance). Garden forks tend to be shorter than pitchforks and have shorter, flatter tines.

Yes, you can find many different kinds of garden forks, though the four-tine model is standard. As with shovels and trowels, pay close attention to what the labels say and ask a store clerk for assistance if you need help determining which type of fork is right for you.

A strong ash or hickory handle is desirable. As for the prongs, they'd better be strong — stamped or forged steel or high-carbon steel, maybe slightly incurved to resist the temptation to bend, with tines that taper to a point. Solid-socket construction where the handle meets the tines is critical because this tool can really take a beating in use, and you don't want it to bend or break.

 You want widely spaced tines so you expend less effort when digging.

Clues to Quality Cultivating Tools

Removing whatever is growing in a spot (whether weeds or wild plants or old lawn, or whatever) creates open ground — which, like a good gardener, you should improve prior to planting (see Chapter 7). So you do everything you're supposed to do, and then what happens? A crust forms. Water may puddle and seedlings may strain to poke through. You need to gently break it up, and that's where cultivating tools come in.

Weeds love freshly cleared ground. They're fast; they're aggressive. They creep in, or birds and other animals deliver them. Seeds that had been slumbering below the surface now have the light, warmth, and moisture they need to sprout. However they arrive, weeds elbow out the plants you want and hog all the resources to boot. What to do? Mulch if you can (see Chapter 7 for details) and cultivate!

Ho, ho, hoes

All sorts of hoes are available, and the one or ones you choose to invest in is partly a matter of what you feel comfortable using and what you need them for. For maximum efficiency, both pushing and pulling action is desirable. At any rate, hoes tend to be long-handled, which is fine, but their blade also needs to be right for the place where you use it. If you'll be working in cramped spaces, like the rows of a vegetable or herb garden, pick a narrow-bladed one, of course. About 6 inches wide is standard.

A good hoe should not be a lightweight or wimpy tool — you mean business. Choose one with a strong, durable hardwood handle (such as hickory or ash). Forged steel is standard for the blade. If either of these parts gets worn out or damaged, replacing it is an option. As for the point of attachment, the handle should be snug and secure in a hole in the top of the blade, even reinforced with rivets, so there's no risk of its falling off.

 Sharpness counts! Your hoe will be sharp when you first bring it home. But you have to keep it so, or else it'll do a sloppy or damaging job. File it often to maintain its beveled edge.

 Hoes do a better job on ground that has recently been watered or rained upon. That's because the weed roots they're meant to be tearing out depart damp ground much more easily and completely than those in dry soil.

Putting an oscillating hoe to use

An *oscillating hoe* (also known as an action hoe, hula hoe, or stirrup hoe) looks different from the average hoe. Rather than a solid piece of sharp metal, it's a shallow open box (like a cookie cutter) of double-edged blades, and it moves about ½ inch back and forth as you push or pull it. Thus, it can cut in two directions and is also self-cleaning (debris slips off with each back-and-forth motion). It's especially effective for combating established weeds in heavy soil.

This sort of hoe is amazingly easy and fun, almost relaxing or hypnotic to use. The stirrups may be as big as 7 inches across or as small as 2 inches across.

Weeding out poor weeders to get to the best

Unlike the hoe, or a layer of smothering mulch or black plastic, a weeder is a hand tool, a clever hand-held weapon in the war on weeds. You can usually take out the invading marauders one at a time. As such, using a weeder is better than attacking the enemy with your bare hands. You can use the same vigor — or frothing rage, if it comes to that! — but a weeding tool makes your efforts more productive. A good weeder helps you extract the entire plant (as you know from dandelions and other weeds, leaving a bit of root behind usually means that the war isn't over yet).

 Just take a look at the many options — try out something — or make an effort to match the weeder to the weed, because some tools are specialists. You need a forked end, for example, to get plants with taproots, and the "mini-hoe"

action of a typical hand weeder works better on shallow-rooted and well-hidden weeds where your aim is merely to slice off the aboveground parts of the plants. I don't find weeders with rotary blades to be very useful.

Because weeders go into the difficult zones of tough soil and tenacious root systems and may contend with daunting obstructions, including rocks and other impediments, they need to be both very tough and somewhat flexible or resilient. Steel is best, of course, though not all steel is created equal. Sturdy gauge steel is fine, and stamped steel is adequate, but if you want a truly powerful and long-lasting weapon, spend your money on a higher-quality forged steel weeder.

 Take out weeds earlier rather than later, because smaller weeds are always easier to attack. Work when the ground is damp from a rain or recent watering, and you should find the job much easier.

Getting a Handle on Hand Pruners

Hand pruners: You should know that many serious gardeners value these handheld cutters above all else — they carry these gadgets everywhere (in a special belt holster or tucked in their back pocket) and are reluctant to lend them. Why? A good pair fits your hand comfortably and takes care of a wide range of gardening jobs, from snipping off the spent stems from last year's perennials to cutting roses for a vase and more. In a word, pruners are handy!

In general, hand pruners are intended for use on anything ½ to ¾ of an inch in diameter (depending on the type) — which covers a lot of gardening cutting jobs, actually.

The best pruner handles are designed to absorb shock but are still lightweight and strong. Usually, they're made of aluminum alloy and coated with a smooth, durable vinyl (usually red!). The more-expensive hand pruners come in left- and right-handed models.

As for the blades, you want tempered carbon steel. It'll start off sharp and need to be resharpened by you or someone else from time to time to maintain the bevel, but it'll hold up well and last a long time. You usually use a whetstone for sharpening, though you may be able to find gadgets made for sharpening pruners that can make the job much easier. Sometimes just replacing nicked up blades is easier. Better hand pruners have replacement cutting blades you can purchase.

Here are some other considerations when you're looking for a good hand pruner:

✔ If you're investing in a good, professional-grade pruner, you may one day want to replace the blades rather than the entire tool, so discern now whether that'll be possible.

A safety latch is very important so the clippers don't spring open when you don't want them to, such as when they're not in use or when they're lodged in your pocket. A good pruner should click in and out of position easily, ideally with a flick of your thumb.

✔ The spring that holds the pivot, keeping it tense, should operate smoothly, without catching, without hesitation. Try it out a few times to make sure.

✔ Some clippers have a nice feature on the bottom blade, a groove that helps carry sap and pitch away from the tool. You should be in the habit of cleaning your pruners after every use anyway, but this little extra certainly helps.

Though you may feel like dozens of different kinds of hand pruners line the store shelves, the tools are really all variations on two themes — bypass pruners and anvil pruners. Both types are approximately the same size but operate differently:

✔ **Bypass pruners:** By far the most common, these pruners make neat, even, shave-close slices, thanks to a beveled cutting blade.

✔ **Anvil-style pruners:** The cutting blade comes down on a slender, non-cutting "anvil" blade, so a flush cut isn't possible. This tool is right for cutting very tough or dead wood. Some anvil-style pruners have a ratcheting action, which makes cutting easier.

Wading through Wondrous Watering Tools

Well, you *know* you need to water your garden, but what you may not know is that you have quite a range of options. If you match the watering tool to the job, your plants will do better and, just as importantly, you won't waste water.

The watering tools in this section are actual tools, not whole watering systems. Most in-ground watering systems should be installed by a professional.

Hoses

The good old garden hose — it saves time and steps.
You can just drag it out to the right spot, turn it on,
let it go, and come back later. Coil it up when it's not
in use. Keep it for years. Simple, right?

Well, not always. Cheap hoses and older ones have
an annoying flaw: They kink and tangle. If you aren't
watching, you can waste water and sometimes harm
plants as the hose lashes around. Then you have the
problem of hoses that crack, burst, and leak after
being left out in the sun or run over by the car, or that
just break down after what seems like not very much
use. Read on for some important considerations when
buying a garden hose.

Materials and construction

The best, most long-lived hose is one that's composed of layers. The inner layer needs to be flexible, a
nice smooth rubber or synthetic tube. To protect it
and give it toughness, it's covered or coated with at
least one outer layer of nylon fabric or mesh. The
outer skin beyond that, the part you touch and see,
needs to be of a material that doesn't break down
after prolonged exposure to sun and weather. It also
needs to resist punctures and scratches. Usually, the
outer layer is vinyl, or a vinyl-rubber blend, and it's
often green or black. Multi-layered hoses may seem a
bit fatter or heavier than the inexpensive alternatives,
but as usual, you get what you pay for.

The standard, vinyl-coated, layered hose comes in different forms: namely three-ply, four-ply, and five-ply.
As with anything, heavier duty versions, like the five-
ply, are more expensive. Heavier duty hoses don't
kink as often, can take higher water pressures, and

last longer. For occasional watering jobs, the lower ply will work fine; for more frequent use and longer life, go with the higher ply.

Other types of hoses include

- **The soaker or leaky hose:** This hose "sweats" water slowly out along its entire length via tiny holes.

- **The flat hose:** Made of cotton canvas, the flat hose is lightweight and compact.

- **The patio hose:** The end of the patio hose is designed to attach to a sink faucet.

The fittings at the ends should also be of good quality. Their job is to attach seamlessly to a faucet (or sprinkler, if at the other end) without leaking or spraying. If they're cast brass rather than cheap metal, they're built to last. A stamped, galvanized steel fitting never seems to hold up over time.

Sizes

The most common hose size is ⅝ of an inch in diameter, which works very well with typical municipal water pressure (30 to 50 pounds per square inch). You may have cause to go down to ½ inch or up to 1 inch — the skinnier one delivers water more slowly; the fatter one, more quickly.

Length depends on how far you have to reach the hose. For flexibility, you may want to buy your hose in 25-foot segments rather than longer lengths and just join them together as needed for different areas of the garden. Also, shorter lengths are lighter and thus easier to lug around.

Storage and placement accessories

Coils and hose caddies are nice accessories to have. You see, a hose comes coiled and stores well coiled in its original direction and loop size — in other words, a hose has *coil memory.* Letting the hose return to this state when not in use is better for the hose's longevity.

A hose guide is a simple but worthwhile gadget. A stake anchors the guide in the ground or in pre-drilled holes in your patio or pathway, and it holds the hose in place, even along curves or around corners. The hose can't stray onto a path or across your garden plants.

Nozzles

A lot of hose accessories are out there. Rarely are they expensive, so you can give one a try and see how you, and your plants, like it. Here are some common ones (they all screw onto the end of a standard hose):

- ✔ **Watering wand:** This gadget extends your reach for watering hanging baskets or irrigating the back of a deep flowerbed. The *rose,* or head, at the end of the wand delivers the water in a gentle, drenching spray. The watering wand is also nice for watering potted plants and seedlings if you keep the water pressure low so you don't dislodge the little plants. Get a wand with a thumb-operated on-off valve so you can move from plant to plant without wetting things you don't mean to or wasting water.

- ✔ **Jet-spray nozzle:** Usually brass, this tool focuses water into a strong, stiff spray. It's ideal for hosing off muddy tools and boots or cleaning a walkway or driveway.

✔ **Adjustable round nozzle:** A refinement of the jet-spray nozzle, this nozzle can also deliver a softer spray right on down to a mist — all by twisting it until the water is coming out the way you want.

✔ **Misting head:** Though small, this tool can be a bit pricier because it usually comes in brass or brass-coated die-cast metal. It delivers water in a fine mist, nice for little emerging seedlings.

✔ **Pistol-grip nozzle:** Usually made of tough, UV-resistant plastic, this nozzle is a favorite among gardeners because you can vary the intensity of the spray by applying pressure to the trigger and thus use it throughout your garden.

✔ **Fan head:** This tool delivers a drenching sweep of water from its broad, broom-head-like end, making it a good choice for bigger watering projects like irrigating a newly planted shrub or rosebush.

✔ **Multiple-head nozzle:** These nozzles have several types of nozzles built into one head and are quite handy.

Hose-end sprinklers

A hose-end sprinkler is designed to screw into a standard hose and rest on the ground wherever you drag it and set it down; it then delivers water in a spray pattern in the immediate area. Clever designers have come up with all sorts of nifty alternatives, so you should have no trouble finding a sprinkler you like and that suits the lay of your particular landscape:

✔ **Fixed-spray sprinkler:** These sprinklers are the simplest types and are perfectly satisfactory for watering small areas. They deliver a fine, soft rain without a super-reliable pattern. Use them on the lawn or for watering flowerbeds and shrubs. You may have to run the water on low or get a heavier model if it tends to flip over on its side or upside down, a common problem.

✔ **Whirlybird sprinkler:** A spring-loaded arm breaks the shooting stream of water into droplets as it snaps back into place, which makes this sprinkler revolve. This deceptively simple design can actually accomplish a very thorough watering job in a circular shape.

✔ **Rain tower:** The rain tower is just an impulse sprinkler like the whirlybird, but it's elevated on an adjustable tripod contraption so it can water a broad circle. It's terrific for watering large areas of tall plants, such as a vegetable garden.

✔ **Oscillating sprinkler:** You have to set or assign these sprinklers their job, which can be a full-yard swing from left to right and back again, or a half-swing to the left or right, or just a held, stationary position. Oscillating sprinklers are marvelous for watering lawns and broad plantings. Splurge on the more expensive units; they last much longer and offer a greater range of settings that can make your watering more accurate and efficient. Compared to a whirlybird sprinkler, oscillating sprinklers tend to lose a lot of water to evaporation.

✔ **Tractor (traveling) sprinkler:** The tractor sprinkler is a little more high-tech, at least for a homeowner. The small water-driven tractor scoots slowly across a lawn, using the laid-out hose as a guide. Meanwhile, a simple revolving sprinkler mounted on top does the watering. Some models have three speeds, for lighter to deeper watering.

Water timers

If you have a good idea how much watering your plants need but don't want to or can't be there, the water timer's for you. Water timers are most often used with professional installed sprinkler systems (which I cover in Chapter 7). Some of these gadgets contain a small computer that you can program for watering time and duration. Others have a clever intermittent feature that delivers the water in on-off cycles (for instance, five minutes on followed by a ten-minute rest) over a period of time (say, three hours) before shutting off automatically. This allows the soil to efficiently absorb the water with far less runoff and evaporation.

One end of the timer attaches to the faucet, the other to the hose end — you have no batteries and no wires to worry about. Some timers are more elaborate (and expensive) than others, so have a clear idea of your needs as well as your technological savvy when you go shopping.

Chapter 5

Growing Annuals and Perennials

• •

In This Chapter
▶ Selecting and purchasing annuals and perennials
▶ Planting annuals and perennials

• •

*F*or sheer flower power, annuals are hard to beat. Because they have to complete their entire life cycle in one growing season — which is the technical definition of the term *annual* — these plants work fast. They go from seed or seedling to full-grown plant, bursting with flowers, in short order, delivering color when and where you need it.

Perennials are meant to last — several years, at least, and sometimes much longer. So ideally, they're a wise and practical "one-time investment," unlike the annuals you have to buy and replant every year.

This chapter can help you choose and place both annuals and perennials in your garden.

Finding Annuals that Fit Your Garden

Modern-day annuals are impressive indeed. They've been bred to produce abundant flowers and lush foliage throughout the heart of the growing season. They rush to flowering because their means of reproduction is by seed. And to get there, the flowers must come first. This great output guarantees bountiful garden color and also makes most annuals great for bouquets. By the time fall comes and seeds form (if they do, before frost), the plants are spent and die. By then, though, you should certainly have gotten your money's worth!

Not surprisingly, a huge range of annuals is on the market, and more annuals arrive every year. The variety of annuals allows you to find countless plants that are specific to warm or cool weather. (For more info about annuals that love sun or shade, check out "Deciding where to plant annuals," later in this chapter.)

Some like it hot: Warm weather annuals

Lots of annuals thrive in hot summer weather, tolerating even periods of prolonged drought. Many annuals have this preference because their predecessors, or ancestors if you will, originated in warm, tropical climates with long growing seasons. All plant breeders did was capitalize on or preserve these qualities while improving the plants' appearance or expanding the color range.

Some warm-weather annuals are actually perennial in some regions but are used as annuals in other areas because they don't survive the winter there. For instance, snapdragon can be a perennial in the South but is used as an annual farther North. Some tropical plants are also commonly used for temporary display.

Examples of favorite warm-weather annuals include impatiens, Madagascar periwinkle, and marigolds.

Some annuals like it cool

Some annuals have their origins in areas with colder winters and mild but not blazingly hot summers. Plant breeders have stepped in to improve these plants' flower production (more blooms), add new colors, and select for compact plant *habit* (shapes or forms). The result is a huge range of good, tough plants that even gardeners with shorter growing seasons can count on. Examples of favorite cool-weather annuals include cleome (spider flower), pansy, Johnny jump-ups (a type of viola), trailing lobelia, and calendula (pot marigolds).

 North or South, cool-loving annuals are often a fine choice for the parts of your garden where shade prevails. The shelter of a fence, pergola (a type of arbor), porch, or overhanging tree keeps the plants cooler, preserving their flower color, prolonging bloom time, and protecting the plants from drying out in the hot sunshine.

Southern summers are generally too hot for cool-season annuals. Enjoy them until late spring and then replace them with something more durable.

Buying Annuals

Because annuals are good for only one growing season, you have to buy new ones each spring. You have two options: seed packets and nursery starts.

Starting with seed packets

The almighty seed is the symbol of a new beginning. Buying your annuals as seed packets gives you four important advantages:

✔ **You can get an earlier start.** Starting seeds indoors takes time and space, but it's not at all difficult.

✔ **Thanks to a broader selection in the seed-packet world, you can grow unusual annuals or new and different colors of popular ones.** Look in seed catalogs that come in late winter, or browse the company Web sites.

✔ **Quantity!** Any given seed packet can contain 100 or more seeds. Even with some attrition, using seed packets is a great way to grow a lot of plants.

✔ **It's inexpensive.** Sure, experienced gardeners bemoan the rising cost of seeds over the years, but, really, it's still the best deal in town, always substantially cheaper than buying young plants.

Be sure to shop early for best selection, and always check the packet to make sure the seeds are fresh. (The packets should be stamped with an expiration date of later this year or next year or should say "packed for [current year]" — see Figure 5-1.) Store the packets in a cool, dry place so the seeds aren't tempted to germinate until you're ready to sow them in flats. For details on how to sow seeds, see Chapter 6.

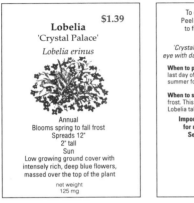

$1.39
Lobelia
'Crystal Palace'
Lobelia erinus

Annual
Blooms spring to fall frost
Spreads 12"
2" tall
Sun
Low growing ground cover with
intensely rich, deep blue flowers,
massed over the top of the plant

net weight
125 mg

To open: Peel this flap back.
Peel back side and bottom flaps
to find additional information
on inside packet!

*'Crystal Palace' Lobelia catches your
eye with dazzling, vibrant, dark blue flowers.*

When to plant outside: Spring after average
last day of frost. In mild winter areas, sow late
summer for winter color.

When to start inside: 8-10 weeks before last
frost. This is the recommended method since
Lobelia takes a long time to germinate.

**Important! Read inside of packet
for more specific information.
See top flap for directions.**

Packed for 2010

7 36210 00011 9

Figure 5-1: Packets of fresh seeds contain planting information, details about the plant, and packing dates.

Starting with nursery, well, starts

You generally see nursery starts at the garden center or home store in mid-to-late spring. Small annual plants are generally sold in six-packs or larger, with each cell holding a single young plant. These plants were raised from seed or from cuttings in a greenhouse and need a little TLC (shelter from cold and wind, regular water so they don't dry out) when you get them home.

Here's what to check before buying:

✔ **Labels:** Labels should contain useful information, such as flower color and mature plant size, as well as the name of the plant.

✔ **Blooms:** A blooming plant may be more attractive, and it lets you check that the color is what you want, but the flowers take energy away from the roots. When you get the plant home, cut or pick off any flowers or buds.

✔ **Well-rooted plants:** Pop or wiggle a plant out and check the rooting. If the seedling promptly falls out of the soil mix, it hasn't been in the cell or pot long enough. If you see a mass of white roots, the plant has been in the cell too long and is stressed.

✔ **Healthy appearance:** Is the foliage crisp and green? Just a few yellowing and bedraggled leaves aren't necessarily a problem — you can pinch those off. But you should look in the crown and the *nodes* (where the leaves or leaf stalks meet the main stem) for insect pests or signs of them.

An Annual Event: The Whens, Wheres, and Hows of Planting

Well, of course, in Northern gardens, annuals bloom in the summer months — and often, they start in spring and don't quit till fall. Lucky gardeners in milder areas with longer growing seasons can enjoy some annuals, especially those that are frost tolerant, year round. Your growing conditions and climate dictate how soon the show gets started, how long it lasts, and where and how you should plant your annuals.

Filling in the garden after the last frost

If you live in an area with a long growing season, you can go ahead and sow annual seeds straight into the ground, secure in the knowledge that they'll sprout, grow up, and start pumping out flowers, all in plenty of time. Gardeners with shorter summers can either start seeds inside or buy seedlings.

Freezing weather kills or at least severely damages most annuals. Therefore, the trick is to know your last spring frost date and your first fall frost date — these dates bookend the annual-gardening year. You can check out Chapter 3 for more information on plant zones and growing seasons.

Planting in late spring

The majority of annuals are frost-sensitive. In other words, a freeze can damage or kill them. Frigid temperatures also make annuals much more susceptible to disease damage. If these small plants are damaged by cold, they may never quite recover. Don't risk it: Plant your new annuals in the ground only after all danger of frost is past. The same goes for plants you're putting in containers (though you can bring the pots indoors on chilly nights if you have to).

 Gardening fever hits us all on the first warm spring day. But warm *air* isn't necessarily what you're waiting for — warm *soil* is. If the ground is still semi-frozen or soggy from thawing cycles or drenching spring rains, wait another week or two. Just remember the wise advice of garden author Roger Swain: Don't put plants in a bed you yourself wouldn't be willing to lie on!

Planting annuals later in the season

Of course you can plant later in the season! Plant and replant all summer long if you want and into fall if you garden in a mild climate. As long as the plants are willing and able to grow and produce flowers, why not?

Because blazing hot weather is stressful, avoid planting during such spells or at least coddle the newcomers with plentiful water and some sheltering shade until they get established. A dose of all-purpose fertilizer (applied according to the instructions and rates on the container) may also hasten latecomers along.

Deciding where to plant annuals

By and large, annuals are resilient plants that tolerate a wide range of growing conditions. But some have preferences for more or less sun, and these specialists allow you to dress up such areas for maximum impact.

Planting in the sun

Full-on, warm sunshine inspires many annuals to grow robustly and generate loads of flowers. You can always tell if a sun-loving annual isn't getting enough light, because its stems become leggy and lean toward the light source, and flower production is disappointing. So let them have it! How much is enough? Six to eight hours a day suits most. My favorite annuals for sun include cosmos, nasturtiums, zinnias, marigolds, and cornflower.

Planting in the shade

Banish gloom in your yard's dim and tree-shaded areas with shade-loving annuals. Plenty do just fine in shade. Indeed, their flowers last longer without the stress of the sun beating down on them. White and yellow flowers really add sparkle, individually or massed. My favorite annuals for shade include tuberous and fibrous begonias, impatiens, and torenia.

Getting annuals in the ground

Annuals are simple to plant. Just follow the label directions for spacing, and dig a hole deeper and wider than the root ball. Add some compost to the hole or mix the native soil with organic matter (see Chapter 7 for details). If desired, you can add some dry fertilizer in the planting hole and water it in, or you can fertilize the annual after planting.

Annuals are most frequently sold in *market packs,* in which six or so plants are each in separate cells. Merely turn the pack upside down and gently push each plant out of its cell from the bottom. Don't pull them out from the top because the stem may break off from the roots. After removing the plants from the packet, plant them in the ground so that their rooting mass is slightly below the soil surface. Firm the soil around the plants and then water them in well.

Looking at Perennials, the Repeat Performers

The broadest definition of a *perennial plant* simply states that it's a *herbaceous,* or nonwoody, plant — as opposed to, say, a shrub or tree — that last a couple years or more. Perennials, like lilies and daffodils, can be bulbs. Herbaceous perennials are plants that have foliage that dies back to the ground, and new foliage and shoots sprout from their overwintering roots next spring.

Perennial plants are a wonderfully varied group, quite possibly the most varied group a gardener can work with. No matter where you live and what your growing conditions are (climate, soil type, sun or shade), you have plenty of plants to choose from. So which perennials should you include in your garden? Start off by knowing which general group can work best for you: hardy perennials or tender perennials.

Hardy perennials

The broad group of hardy perennials is justly popular in colder climates (they're generally appropriate for gardens in USDA Zones 3–8 — see Chapter 3 for details on hardiness zones). These plants emerge each spring, producing foliage and flowers. Come fall, their top growth dies down and the show is over for the year. But the roots live on underground, waiting to revive and do it all again when warm weather returns.

Popular examples of hardy perennials include aster, columbine, coneflower, day lily, delphinium, mums, penstemon, peony, phlox, and Shasta daisy.

Tender perennials

Contrary to popular belief, the upper parts of the Northern Hemisphere don't have the corner on perennials. Lots of plants from milder climes (say, USDA Zones 8, 9, 10, and warmer, right on into the tropics) meet the perennial description. These repeat performers burst forth in warm spring weather, enjoy the summer months, and slow down or die down in the fall, roots still very much alive. They return in glory when the year cycles around to springtime again.

Obviously, you can grow tender perennials with impunity if you're in a mild-climate area. However, everyone else can enjoy them, too: Gardeners just have to get the tender treasures through winter, because these plants can't tolerate or survive cold temperatures. Or certainly, you can leave your tender perennials in the garden to perish over the winter — which makes them, essentially, annuals and means you may ending up buying new ones next spring.

Popular examples of tender perennials include angelonia, coleus, gerbera, impatiens, and pentas.

Finding and Buying Perennials

If you have a clear idea of which plants you want, you're ready to go get them. You can acquire a perennial plant in many different ways, but I cover the most common methods in this section.

To the market: Getting perennials in containers

You can usually purchase partially grown perennials in pots, and they come in a variety of pot sizes, from a mere 2 inches on up to 5 gallons. Both mail-order nurseries and local retailers sell perennials in containers (see the next section for info on mail-order perennials). The larger the plant is, the more mature — and expensive — it is, and the more immediate your gratification; a smaller plant can catch up quickly if you plant it in an appropriate site and give it good care. Consider also how big of a hole you want to dig.

Here are some important ideas to remember so you can be sure of getting a good potted plant:

✔ **Buy a healthy plant.** Examine the entire plant. Look above and below the leaves as well as along the stems for signs of insect or disease damage. A few yellowing leaves are fine.

Examine the crown for signs of rot (no good, obviously) and fresh new shoots (very good).

Pop the plant out of its pot and examine the roots. They should be crisp and viable, often white or brown. Avoid pot-bound plants.

✔ **Choose a plant that's not yet in bloom.** Some growers force plants into early bloom so they'll look good at the stores, but don't be seduced! The trip home in your car or adjusting to the transplanting process often causes blossoming perennials to jettison expendable growth; in other words, they ditch petals and unfurling buds.

If your new plant sheds its flowers on the way home, make sure you plant the perennial well and care for it; it may bloom again soon enough. However, many perennials don't rebloom, so the show may be over until next year. You're best off choosing a plant that's conserving its energy.

✔ **Don't buy out of season.** Bargain perennials aren't always a bargain. Those plants for sale in midsummer have a stressful time of establishing themselves; fall-planted ones may do just fine or may succumb to winter's cold.

✔ **Have alternatives in mind.** You can't always get what you want, but with all your options, you should be able to find something that works.

Buying perennials through mail-order

Buying through mail-order can be very convenient. You can shop from a catalog or on a Web site in the dead of winter or in the middle of the night in your jammies. Also, you can spend plenty of time thinking over your plans. After all, mail-order companies often carry a broader range of varieties than local providers do. And you get your plants delivered to your door at the right time to be planted — all without standing in line! Just make sure you pick out a company that's been in business for a while, that's able to answer your phone or e-mail questions, and that your gardening friends have had good experiences with.

This section outlines how plants may look after their trip. Check out "Preparing for the actual planting" for info on how to treat the plants after they arrive.

Potted plants, ready for action

Some mail-order nurseries ship small perennials in small pots. If you get a live-plant shipment, open it immediately upon arrival, even if you're not going to plant anything that very day. Inspect the plants as I describe in the preceding section, and quarantine any plants of questionable quality. Call the nursery immediately if you see a problem so you can work out a refund, merchandise credit, or replacement.

Small potted plants aren't necessarily baby perennials. Such young plants take too long to grow, and mail-order nurseries want you to jump right in and enjoy your garden. So the small plants nurseries ship out tend to be 2-year-old, field-grown plants that have simply had a "haircut" of the top growth prior to shipping. A good, strong root system is just what you want. Don't worry: Fresh, new top growth will soon follow!

Their roots are showing: Dormant, bareroot perennials

Bareroot perennials are the typical mail-order product. Selling perennials this way is simply more practical for some plants for a variety of reasons. For instance, baby's breath and baptisia have root systems that are sensitive to being moved in and out of the ground and various pots too many times. Other perennials, like day lilies and peonies, have large roots systems that don't fit well in smaller pots. These bareroot plants are also dormant and lightweight, which makes shipping cheaper and less risky.

Like potted mail-order plants, bareroot ones are usually 2-year-old, field-harvested plants. They were probably dug up the previous fall, just as they became dormant, and kept in climate-controlled cold storage until spring-shipping season. Bareroot plants consist of a hearty root system and some trimmed-down stems; little or no leaf growth should be evident.

Acquiring free divisions

Usually, free divisions from other gardeners are surplus plants, which means that these plants have been growing well in their garden of origin. This is good news for you —the plants are in good health, and that sort of plant probably thrives in your area.

You can also obtain divisions from mature plants already growing in your yard if you're creating a new gardening bed or expanding an old one.

Planting Perennials

Perennials are probably the hottest topic these days among garden enthusiasts and plant suppliers. As a result, information about how to select and plant them abounds. Reputable garden centers have knowledgeable salespeople, and universities, garden centers, and public libraries sponsor various workshops and lecture programs about them. If you need more information than you find in the sections ahead, check out these sources and the books in your public library or local bookstore.

Figuring out where to plant perennials

Good news — there's a perennial for almost any growing situation your yard can dish up. Make a match between the conditions you have to offer and the known characteristics of a plant, and you're halfway there. A little care from you on planting day and beyond, and your perennials are sure to thrive.

Sunny locations

Lots of perennials adore sunshine. They grow more compactly when they get enough sun (as opposed to becoming lanky or leaning towards the light source), and they produce more and better flowers.

Full sun means six or more hours per day. If you have to choose between a spot with morning sun and a spot with afternoon sun, most sun-loving perennials seem to do better with the afternoon site. This situation varies somewhat on your climate. If you live in the deep South, a plant that grows best in full sun in a Northern climate may perform better in a spot protected from hot, late afternoon sun.

Because sun can be drying, either choose dryland natives or help out the plants with regular watering and a moisture-conserving mulch around their root systems.

Favorite sun perennials include artemisia, armeria, basket-of-gold, blanket flower, coneflower, coreopsis, delphinium, gaura, lavender, penstemon, peony, sea holly, and yarrow.

Shady spots

Many perennials prefer shade, prospering in a range of conditions ranging from deepest woodland gloom to areas of dappled or filtered light to those that get morning sun and afternoon shade.

Not only that, but many plants appropriate for shade have beautiful leaves — you can find amazing variety in shape, texture, and even color. And you may be pleasantly surprised to hear that plenty of shade plants produce attractive flowers.

Shade is actually a benefit to many plants. Lack of direct sun means their leaves look healthy and lush, without burned edges or tips, without drying out or wilting. Sunlight also tends to bleach out the beauty of variegated leaves (leaves that are marked or rimmed in white, cream, or gold), whereas in shade, such foliage thrives and lights up the scene. Shelter from the sun's hot rays also preserves flower color.

Favorite shade perennials include ajuga, astilbe, bergenia, bleeding heart, brunnera, coral bells, corydalis, many ferns, goatsbeard, hellebore, hosta, lady's mantle, lamium, lily-of-the-valley, lungwort, Solomon's seal, and sweet woodruff.

Dry soil

If sandy, gritty, or fast-draining soil is your lot, a fabulous perennial garden is still possible. Sure, digging in some organic matter at planting time (and on an annual basis) is good advice that you should follow when you can, but your gardening life can be a lot easier if you go native. You don't have to pour on water you don't have, and you may be delighted with the easy maintenance and attractive look.

Peruse the offerings at a local nursery that specializes in indigenous plants. Visit a public garden or botanic garden with displays of natives. *Your eyes will be opened.* Botanists and horticulturists feel your pain and have been working hard over the years to find out which ones adapt best to gardens and which ones are prettiest. There are even selections or cultivated varieties (cultivars) that are significant improvements over their wild parents — new flower colors and bigger, longer-lasting flowers on more-compact, handsome plants.

Favorite dry-soil perennials include black-eyed Susan, blanket flower, baptisia, butterflyweed, evening primrose, gaura, penstemon, phormium (a tender perennial in most regions), and yarrow. And don't overlook cacti and succulents — a well-stocked local or mailorder nursery can convince of their astounding range and beauty.

Wet soil

Soggy, boggy ground is usually written off as a lost area or liability. But what if that damp side yard, wet back forty, or perpetually muddy roadside ditch were to come alive with handsome leaves and blooming color? It's certainly possible. A host of plants actually like wet feet; a little research can point you to the ones that are a match for your problem-spot's conditions.

You may have to wade in prior to planting and get the spot ready. Bring your rubber boots and create a hospitable open area with gusto and determination! Yank out most or all the existing vegetation so it doesn't compete with the desirable incoming perennials. If warranted and practical, dig a drainage trench to route excess water away from the spot. Perhaps dig in some organic matter to improve soil fertility and drainage.

After you've planted the area with appropriate moisture-loving perennials, not much more should be required. The plants' basic need — water — is already present. If the plants are happy, they'll increase over time, reducing the need for weeding or indeed, any intervention on your part. If they grow too lushly, you can rip out and discard or give away the extra plants.

Cardinal flower, day lilies, forget-me-not, Japanese primrose, marsh marigold, and turtlehead are good plants for wet soil.

Clay soil: Soggy soil at its worst

Slick and soggy in wet weather and nearly impenetrable in dry, clay soil is actually composed of lots of densely packed, very tiny particles. Clay leaves little space for air and water to circulate, and the result is heavy ground that drains poorly. Needless to say, many perennials — or rather, their roots — have a hard go of it in such conditions.

Clay soil does have some advantages, believe it or not. It's often fairly fertile because it holds nutrients and water so well. And of course, it's slower to dry out in hot weather, which can help your plants.

At any rate, if clay is your lot in life, you have three options:

✔ **Improve the soil's structure.** Add organic matter. Doing so can help lighten and aerate the area, making it more hospitable to perennials and other plants and allowing water to drain away better. Dig organic matter in often and deeply — compost and/or well-rotted manure are up to the job. (For details on soil improvement, check out Chapter 7.)

✔ **Go with what you have.** Plant clay-tolerant perennials, such as beebalm, cardinal flower, chrysogonum, epimedium, many ferns, galax, gunnera, Japanese iris, Japanese primrose, marsh marigold, or myosotis.

✔ **Bypass it.** Grow your perennials in raised beds (see Chapter 6) or pots.

Deciding when to plant perennials

Perennials tend to be rather tough and forgiving plants in terms of picking the right time to plant them, but generally, most people plant perennials in either the spring or the fall.

Perhaps the best way to know when to plant perennials is to know when *not* to plant them. For example, avoid planting perennials in stressful conditions, or you will, as the saying goes, reap what you sow. No-no times include

✔ Any blazing hot day

✔ Any time of drought

✔ Any time when frost is predicted

✔ Any time when the ground is soggy or still frozen

✔ Right after a deluging storm or flood

Spring planting

Springtime is the preferred time to plant perennials for good reason. All the conditions these plants relish and respond to are in place: warming soil, warm sunshine, longer days, moist ground, and regular rainfall. Roots quest into the ground, taking up water and nutrients to fuel growth, and *top growth* — foliage, stems, and flowers — surges forth.

When getting ready for spring planting, make sure you do the following:

1. **Harden the plants off.**

   Let new plants adjust to life outdoors for a few days or a week by sitting them in a sheltered spot, such as on the porch or against the semi-shady side of the house. Start the plants off for just a few hours, and increase the time until they're outdoors 24/7. (But bring perennials indoors or cover them if there's a threat of a late frost.) Cover them with single layer of newspaper to reduce the light intensity and wind exposure.

2. **Choose a cool, cloudy, or damp day to plant, or plant in late afternoon.**

   The hottest part of the day (midday to early afternoon) is a bit stressful to both you and the plants!

3. **Plant in good soil, create a basin of soil or mulch around each plant, and give a good, soaking watering.**

   Check that the water drains in where you want it.

4. **Mulch after planting.**

   Not only does this step hold in soil moisture and moderate the effects of fickle, fluctuating spring temperatures, but it also keeps weeds at bay.

Here are some things perennials find very unpleasant. During spring planting, do not

✔ **Handle the plants roughly.**

✔ **Plunk a root-bound plant into the ground.**
Either tease apart the roots a bit or lightly score the sides with a sharp knife, which inspires new root growth. *Then* you may place the perennial in its planting hole.

✔ **Plant perennials in waterlogged ground, or drench them right after planting.** A moderate dose of water is a needed drink; too much water prohibits oxygen from getting to the roots, and the plants literally drown or rot.

Fall planting

Autumn turns out to be a fine time to plant many perennials in temperate climates. The soil and air are cooler now and sunlight is less intense, so the weather's less stressful for newcomer plants. Competition from weeds isn't likely to be a big problem, either.

In some regions, rainfall becomes more regular, too, which helps provide the moisture the perennials need to start good root growth. And their roots *do* grow — the plants simply aren't programmed to start producing lots of new leaves or flowers at this time of year. Yes, the perennials will soon head into winter dormancy, but fall planting often gives these perennials a head start over their spring-planted counterparts.

When spring rolls around, you may notice the difference. The fall-planted perennials should be raring to grow, larger and more robust. You can expect a good show. All this, plus you won't have to elbow through crowds at the garden center.

Fall planting also applies to perennials you want to dig up and move to a new spot and to *divisions* (strong, rooted pieces of overgrown plants).

When getting ready for fall planting, make sure you do the following:

- ✔ Buy good, strong plants. These plants have the best chance to establish themselves in your garden.

- ✔ Mulch a little at planting time, about ½ to 1 inch, to hold in soil moisture and warmth; mulch even more as winter arrives, another 2 or 3 inches after the ground freezes, to protect the plants during the cold months. (For more info on mulching options, see Chapter 7.)

- ✔ Cut back the top growth, just to further urge the plant to concentrate on root growth.

Here are some things to *avoid* during fall planting:

- ✔ **Fertilizing:** Fertilizing inspires a fresh spurt of young shoots and leaves, which are vulnerable to cold damage. You want perennials to enter their winter dormancy.

- ✔ **Plant late-bloomers:** Late bloomers (like asters, mums, black-eyed Susan, and perennial ornamental grasses) are better planted in spring.

Make doubly sure, before you find out the hard way, which plants relish fall planting and which do not. You can always double check at wherever you buy perennials in the fall. Reputable nurseries don't sell plants that resent being planted this time of year. Some fall-planting favorites are day lilies, peonies, oriental poppies, and rhizomatous iris.

Preparing for the actual planting

How to plant your perennials has a lot to do with how you acquired them, whether by mail-order, from the local nursery, or as a division from a fellow gardener.

If you purchased your plants mail-order as pots or bare roots, here's what to do when they're delivered:

1. **Unpack immediately, and inspect the plants.**

   As with potted ones, you want to be on the look-out for obvious problems of pests or rot. And you want to see crisp roots. You shouldn't see any green stem or leaf growth yet, or at least not much.

2. **Hold the plants in a cool, dark place until you're ready to plant them — perhaps for a few days or a week at the most.**

   The refrigerator is also fine. Mist them lightly if they seem dry.

   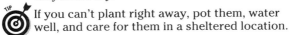 If you can't plant right away, pot them, water well, and care for them in a sheltered location.

3. **On planting day, rehydrate the roots by soaking them in a bucket of tepid water for a few hours.**

Here's how to handle plant divisions:

- ✔ **Keep plant divisions moist.** Don't let them dry out! This idea is especially important if you're not prepared to plant the divisions in your garden right away. Place them in a plastic bag or box and sprinkle on some water or temporarily pot them; water well.

- ✔ **Clean them up.** Clip off or tug out weeds and limp, yellowing, or damaged foliage. Cut off flowering stalks (don't worry, they'll generate new ones soon enough). Right now, you just want the divisions to devote their energy to establishing their roots in your yard.

✔ **Plant in a prepared area and keep an eye on them.** Don't just toss divisions on the ground and hope for the best, even if your friend characterized them as tough guys. They need time, water, and weeding to get their legs under them.

See the preceding section for seasonally specific planting tips. For advice on planting perennials that come from a local store or supplier, please review the planting instructions for annuals that I provide earlier in this chapter.

Chapter 6

Food, Glorious Food! Growing Your Own Veggies

- -

In This Chapter

▶ Looking at veggies and vegetable-garden fruits

▶ Getting seeds and transplants

▶ Preparing your bed, sowing seeds, and planting

- -

*F*or the cost of a packet of seeds, you can have your own homegrown produce. The requirements are simple: good soil, moisture, and full sun. This type of gardening is usually called vegetable gardening, even though it also involves growing items that are technically fruit, such as tomatoes and melons. Growing your own produce — or vegetables, as it were — can be fun and fairly easy for the beginner gardener. This chapter gives you the basics. If you want even more information, please check out *Vegetable Gardening For Dummies* (Wiley).

Varieties of Veggies

Lots of wonderful and worthwhile types of vegetables are available — too many to list, really, but they're fun to explore. Read this section with the goal of figuring out what you may want to grow where you live. Favor vegetables that are too expensive at the store or never available locally. Treat yourself to new foods or enticing variations on old standbys.

Days to maturity refers to the time elapsed between sowing a seed and picking the harvest for those veggies that are directly sown. Something like a radish or mesclun salad mix can accomplish this in 30 days or less. For plants that are normally grown from transplants, like peppers and tomatoes, the maturity time dates from when the small plants are planted in the ground until they bear.

Generally speaking, varieties of the same vegetable are ready at around the same time, give or take a few days. If you have a big gap, there's an explanation. For instance, 'Easter Egg' radish is ready in 25 days, but 'Summer Cross' takes 45 days because it's one of those giant white Oriental daikon types.

Please note that the days-to-maturity figure is relative — it's a prediction. Results vary according to your climate and the conditions in your garden.

Growing vegetables by seasons

Matching your vegetables to your season length is sensible advice. If your growing season is approximately 90 days, growing anything billed as maturing in that amount of time or less ought to be easy. If you push the envelope, be prepared to help that variety with an early start indoors or some extra coddling in the fall. With experience, you can find out what you can and are willing to do.

First, though, get an idea of the growing seasons that you have to contend with (for info on growing seasons, see Chapter 3). Typically, the vegetable-gardening season is summer, bookended by late spring and early fall. Gardeners mark the start by the last spring frost date and the finish by the first fall frost date (although some crops, like parsnips and kale, can stay out in the cold a bit longer and even gain improved flavor).

If your growing season is long and warm, you can get started earlier and maybe even plant two or three rounds of crops. You may, however, have to contend with hot, dry weather at the height of summer, which is stressful for some vegetable crops (so mulch them and supply extra water).

If your growing season is short, you can still have a very bountiful vegetable garden. Choose vegetables that mature faster, and try some season-extending tricks:

- ✔ Start seeds early indoors or in a cold frame, which is basically a box made of such materials as wood or concrete blocks covered with a glass or plastic sash that protects smaller plants from extreme cold and wind. Raising them to seedling-size until putting them out in the ground is safe. (See the upcoming section "Starting your own seeds indoors.")

- ✔ Use plastic coverings (from row-cover sheeting or tunnels to cones to recycled milk jugs to "water wall" wraps) to keep a plant and its immediate soil nice and warm.

You can grow some vegetables during the winter. Yes. Really! In mild climates, you can enjoy kale, carrots, leeks, and root vegetables all winter long. You may have to mulch them and then poke under to harvest but, hey, it's worth it! You can even sow salad greens in October and harvest extra-early in spring. Mmm.

Table 6-1 gives an overview of which vegetables tend to do better during which seasons.

Table 6-1	Ideal Seasons for Growing Vegetables	
Type	*Description*	*Examples*
Cool-season vegetables	These plants tolerate some frost and temperatures between 55 and 70°F. As such, they're fine choices for gardeners in more northern areas or, in milder climates, for growing in a cool spring or fall.	Asparagus, beets, broccoli, Brussels sprouts, cabbage, carrot, cauliflower, collard, endive, kale, kohlrabi, lettuce, onion, Oriental greens, parsnip, peas, potato, radish, Swiss chard, spinach, turnip, and turnip greens
Warm-season vegetables	These plants are readily harmed by frost; they also fare poorly in cold soil. Grow these plants in temperatures ranging from 65 to 80°F. They're good in the South and West and elsewhere during the height of summer.	Beans, corn, cucumber, eggplant, melons (muskmelon/cantaloupe, watermelon), pepper, sweet potato, pumpkin, squash, sweet corn, and tomato

Type	Description	Examples
Perennials	These edible plants live from one year to the next, typically producing good crops their second or third seasons and thereafter. You can grow them in most climates, providing a protective winter mulch if warranted.	Asparagus and rhubarb

Defining hybrids

You may see the term *hybrid* on seed packets and in seed catalogs. All it means is that the vegetable variety in question is a result of a cross (through pollination) between two parent plants of the same species but different subspecies or varieties.

Uniformity, predictability, and disease resistance are the results of combining the genetic traits of two good parents and repeating the same cross. Hybrid offspring are often more robust and productive than either parent. Something called *hybrid vigor* often appears, a healthy exuberance that seems to result from the good qualities of one parent canceling out the bad of the other.

What's the catch? Actually, I can name two. Producing hybrid seed requires the seed company to maintain the two parent lines and often to laboriously hand-pollinate, so hybrid seeds are more expensive than the alternative (see "Appreciating heirlooms"). Also, there's no point in saving seed from a hybrid that you like and replanting it next year — it won't be the same and may exhibit various mongrel qualities from either of its parents.

Favorite hybrid vegetables include 'Big Boy' beefsteak tomato, 'Blushing Beauty' bell peppers, 'Nantes' carrot, 'Salad Bowl' leaf lettuce, 'Silver Queen' sweet corn, and 'Crenshaw' cantaloupe melon.

Appreciating heirlooms

Heirloom vegetables are vegetable varieties that people save and pass on for more-practical home-gardener virtues such as excellent flavor and a pro-longed harvest period. Commercial seed companies, on the other hand, breed for uniformity as well as good shipability (thicker, tougher skins on tomatoes and squash, for instance) and ripening-all-at-once (for harvesting convenience).

When a variety is called "open pollinated," it means the seeds are the result of natural pollination by insects or wind. With veggies that have open-pollinated seeds (on-hybrid varieties), you can save the seeds and plant them again next year; they'll be the same. Heirloom varieties are simply those that have been passed down through generations of gardeners, like any other family heirloom. Older ones that are still in circulation have stood the test of time and should be worthwhile.

Specialty seed catalogs have wonderful selections (do an Internet search or comb the ads in gardening magazines and send for the catalogs). Many mainstream catalogs are offering more heirloom vegetables in response to demand. You can also nose around your neighborhood gardeners, community gardens, and/or farmer's markets to meet other like-minded gardeners who can share their seeds and knowledge of them.

What's the catch with heirlooms? Well, they're not as perfect or uniform-looking. Because heirlooms aren't commercially bred, they may be more colorful and more variable in size and shape than their hybrid counterparts. Also, their skins may be thinner, so you get great flavor, but they don't travel well and may be vulnerable to bruising — or they may have lots of seeds inside (as in certain squashes and pumpkins), causing you a bit of extra work to separate out the edible parts.

Favorite heirloom vegetable varieties include 'Moon and Stars' watermelon, 'Tom Thumb' baby butterhead lettuce, 'Gold Nugget' winter squash, 'Ragged Jack' kale, 'Super Italian Paste' tomato, 'Henderson's Bush' lima bean, and 'French Breakfast' spring radish.

Getting Your Vegetable Garden Ready

Most produce is, of course, grown in a vegetable garden, and it's always best to get your garden started before even acquiring your plants. Of course, you have to dig into the soil and work in organic matter. One of the first steps, however, is designing your garden.

Sketching out your plan

The best planning advice is simple: Start small. Just be sure you locate in a spot where expansion is possible, should you want to make a bigger garden in ensuing years. As for actual size, it depends on what you want to grow. Just to give you a general idea, here's what you can put in the following standard-size gardens:

- ✔ A 6 × 8 foot plot can support a couple of tomato plants, maybe some bush beans, and some lettuce.

- ✔ A 10 × 18 foot plot can hold all that, plus a couple of space-consuming squash plants and cucumbers, and maybe some carrots or beets.

- ✔ A 20 × 24 foot plot can hold all that, plus peppers, leeks, broccoli, turnips, and maybe some herbs as well.

- ✔ A 40 × 60 plot allows you more of everything, plus some bigger items, such as asparagus and rhubarb.

Sketch out your vegetable garden plan on paper ahead of time. Figure out how much space to allot to individual plants — and don't forget to allow for space between the rows, or paths, so you can tend the plants. (Mature sizes of various vegetable varieties are noted on seed packets and often in catalog descriptions.)

Working with the sun: Where to plant vegetables

Most fruiting vegetables like the environment sunny and open — the soil is warm, light is plentiful, and they grow easily, developing and ripening their fruit with minimal stress or impediments. Examples of sun-loving vegetables include tomatoes, peppers, squash, beans, okra, eggplant, and corn.

 To maximize needed sun, site your vegetable garden in a south-facing spot; plant taller plants to the north end so they don't cast shade over their shorter fellows.

Some vegetables are less dependent on full sun, which can fade or dry out their foliage or slow their growth. Or the plants may just may like cooler temperatures. Vegetables that gardeners grow for their leaves fall into this group, as do ones with edible roots. Examples include lettuce, mixed greens (mesclun), chard, potatoes, carrots, and turnips.

To maximize sheltering shade, grow these vegetables in an east- or west-facing garden; site taller plants and objects (including trellises, teepees, and caged or staked tomatoes) in front of and to the south of these shade-lovers. Or grow these plants earlier in spring or in the fall — assuming you have enough time to ripen them before winter comes, that is.

Using planting patterns and systems

As much as you may like to toss a packet of seeds into a pile of dirt and let the plants grow where they fall, you may be better off working with some kind of system. This section explains how you can design around a natural garden, raised beds, or existing landscaping.

Natural garden beds

Natural garden beds can be in-ground or mounded up, without need of wooden edges. Either way, work the soil between 8 and 12 inches deep to accommodate the roots of most vegetables.

Natural beds don't need any kind of edging, but you do need to remove the sod if you're turning part of the lawn into a garden. It is best to remove the sod with a sod knife (a special tool that can be rented) or a spade. For larger jobs, you can rent a sod cutter, which is a machine that penetrates the soil about three inches deep and cuts off the roots of the sod. It can then be rolled up and removed. For smaller jobs, you can rent a manual sod cutter or you can use a spade.

It is important to remove the sod and then rototill. Don't try to rototill over the grass. Only larger rototillers are capable of doing this, and if you till in the grass, it will be impossible to completely remove the grass and it will constantly re-sprout — a real pain!

As far as other weeds go, remove as many as you can before you till or work up the soil. When new ones sprout, remove them as soon as possible — when they are young and before they produce more weeds!

More ambitious vegetable gardens need plenty of paths and rows to allow access — for you, for a hose, for a wheelbarrow. Ideally, you want access from all four sides of a particular bed. Build pathways into your master plan when you're first sketching out the layout. Then, to clarify where the paths are and also to prevent weeds from seizing the open space, "pave" the paths with a layer of straw (not hay), dried grass clippings, or gravel.

Raised garden beds

Using raised garden beds is a very practical way to construct a good vegetable garden. They have good drainage, the soil warms up quickly in the spring, they're easy to weed (high off the ground), and you're less likely to step on and compact the soil, so roots can grow better in looser, well aerated ground. Just make bottomless wooden boxes between 8 and 12 inches deep, set them in a sunny, flat area, fill with good soil, and away you go. Native soil can be used if it's of good quality; otherwise half native and half added purchased soil would work fine. See Figure 6-1 for how to build a raised bed. If you use more than one raised bed, space them so you can walk between them or bring a wheelbarrow down the row. Construction tip: Brace each corner with a corner post for extra stability.

Figure 6-1: Making a raised bed. First build up the earth for planting (A). Then plant your garden and put up the wooden walls to contain everything. This prevents you from damaging your garden during planting.

Note that the wood you use should be untreated lumber. Treated wood may leach harmful preservatives, which is not a risk you want to take when raising edibles. Rot-resistant redwood or cedar is great; other softwoods, including pine, tamarack, and cypress, can also do but tend to rot away after a few years and need replacing.

 If tunneling rodents are an issue where you garden, keep them out of your raised bed by lining the bottom with a layer of chicken wire. Use a slightly-too-big piece so you can pull it partway up the sides and tack or staple it in place.

Prepping your soil

The biggest mistake beginning vegetable gardeners make is using lousy or too-thin soil. If you're working with a brand-new vegetable garden (or one that fell fallow and you're bringing it back to life), I suggest you stake it out and get it ready the autumn before you plan to plant. This act gives the soil and the amendments you've added time to settle and meld. It also means you have less work to do next spring.

If a fall start isn't possible or practical, go ahead and prepare the ground in spring — but don't start too early. If the ground is still semifrozen or soggy, digging in the soil can compact it and harm its structure. How do you tell whether it's ready to be worked in? Grab a handful and squeeze — it should fall apart, not form a mud ball.

Follow these steps when preparing your soil:

1. **Dig deep.**

   Most vegetables are content with 6 to 8 inches of good ground for their roots to grow in. If you're planning to grow substantial root crops (potatoes, say, or carrots), go deeper still — up to a foot or more.

2. **Fill 'er up.**

   Add lots and lots of organic matter! Try compost, dehydrated cow manure, shredded leaves, well-rotted horse manure (call nearby stables), or a mixture thereof. If your yard has fertile soil, adding organic matter is less crucial, but most soils can stand the improvement. Mix it with the native soil, fifty-fifty, or even more liberally.

Maybe your area's soil is notoriously acidic, or very sandy, or quite obviously lousy for plant growth. The good news is that organic matter can be like a magic bullet in that it helps improve whatever you add it to. You have to replenish the organic matter at the start of every growing season or maybe even more often. If the soil stubbornly resists improvement, resort to setting raised beds atop it and filling these bottomless boxes with excellent, organically rich soil.

Finding Your Vegetables

Generally, most gardeners buy their vegetables as seed packets or as young transplants or container plants. People often purchase plants and seeds in the spring from a variety of places, including markets, home stores, and nurseries. You'll notice different brands and companies and frankly, not huge differences in price.

Whether you choose to grow plants from seed or buy started plants may depend on cost, the kind of selection you want, when you want to begin, and the type of plant.

Buying seeds

Seed packets are particularly popular because they help save money and provide a broader, more interesting selection. Upon purchase, or certainly upon opening a new seed packet, you quickly notice an awful lot of little seeds in there! The reasons are many: The company wants to make you feel as though you're getting something substantial for your money, and when you sow, some won't sprout or will be thinned out later.

You also get enough for successive sowings or to save for next year (little seeds, like lettuce seeds, tend to dry out if stored for a year, whereas big seeds like beans can keep for several years). Keep seeds in a dry, cool (non-freezing) place until you're ready to sow them.

Certain seeds can, and should, be started indoors, well before the garden outside is awake yet — so read the labels to see whether indoor starting or *direct-sowing* (sowing outside, when the soil and weather is warm enough) is recommended for the area where you live. ("Sowing and planting your veggies" has more info.)

Buying nursery transplants

You can purchase transplants, container plants, or seedlings locally — at a garden center, home store, farmer's market, spring fair, or from roadside entrepreneurs — or from mail-order companies. Someone else has done the seed-starting work for you; all you have to do is choose, take 'em home, and care for them. If you can't get the plants into the ground right away, set them in a sheltered spot out of the hot sun and the wind and water them often.

Transplants are the way to go if you can't or don't want to bother with seed-starting, or if you wait till the last minute to decide what you're growing this year. They're worth the upcharge for the convenience.

Just as with seed-shopping, you can shop for different varieties (buy three different kinds of tomatoes, for example). Again, though, the selection may not be too exciting comparatively.

Ones to buy pre-started include tomatoes, peppers, and eggplants. Certain vegetables simply don't transplant well from a wee pot to the garden. Direct-sow plants like corn, carrots, and potatoes.

Of course, you can also create your own transplants from your own seeds. I explain how under "Starting your own seeds indoors," later in this chapter.

Planting Your Vegetables

When getting ready to plant, the first rule is to pay attention to which items are cool-season vegetables and which are warm-season vegetables (see the earlier section "Growing vegetables by seasons"). You can start cool-season vegetables earlier and put them in the ground earlier because they're more tolerant of cooler temperatures (some can even go outdoors before the last frost). However, you should put warm-season vegetables out or sow them only after all danger of frost is past. After you figure out which veggies are which in your planting plans, you're ready to determine when to start planting. And then, of course, you're ready to plant!

Deciding when to plant your veggies

The date of the last frost is the date when you're free to plant vegetable seedlings or direct-sow vegetable seeds into the garden. The last frost date is in late spring, but the date varies from year to year. You can find out down at the local garden center or from the nearest office of the Cooperative Extension Service.

When to plant transplants

If you have seedlings ready to go into the garden after the soil is ready and sufficiently warmed up — seedlings of your own or ones you've bought — your garden can get off to an earlier start. In the final analysis, your garden will be more productive this year! Vegetables that you can start early indoors include cabbage, tomatoes, peppers, and eggplant.

If you start too early, your seedlings may be too big too early, making them a little hard to accommodate and care for — you may even have to start over. Here's a general list to get you started; you can tinker as you get more experience raising various seeds. Yep, get out your calendar — some counting backwards is in order:

- **Onions:** 12 to 14 weeks before the safe planting-out day (which in the case of onions is 4 to 6 weeks before the last frost)

- **Broccoli, collards, and cabbage:** 5 to 6 weeks before the safe planting-out date (which is after the danger of snow and ice is past but while nights are still chilly)

- ✔ **Lettuce:** 5 to 6 weeks before the safe planting-out day (which is 4 to 5 weeks before the last frost)
- ✔ **Peppers:** 8 to 12 weeks before the last frost
- ✔ **Tomatoes and eggplant:** 6 to 8 weeks before the last frost
- ✔ **Cucumbers and melons:** 2 to 4 weeks before the last frost

When to sow seeds directly

Gardeners generally sow seeds directly in the garden after the last frost, after the soil has warmed up and the weather seems to have settled into an early-summer groove. Direct-sowing in cold and/or soggy soil is a bad idea — it's muddy work for you, and the seeds usually sprout poorly or rot; then you have to start over.

Vegetables that you can direct-sow include lettuce, onions, peas, radishes, turnips, beets, cabbage, carrots, beans, corn, parsnips, cucumber, lettuce, and tomatoes (in warm climates).

Sowing and planting your veggies

How to plant vegetables really depends on the form in which you've acquired them. Do you want to plant seeds, or do you want to plant transplants that you've acquired? Or do you want to combine both approaches and create your own transplants from seeds? Here I give you information on all three approaches.

Starting your own seeds indoors

A sure way to banish the winter blues, as well as get a jumpstart on your vegetable garden, is to start some seeds indoors early. To find out how early, consult the back of the seed packet; you want to time it so you have several-inch-high seedlings in late spring, after the danger of frost in your area has passed. Refer to Figure 6-2 and follow these steps:

1. **Select a good spot.**

   In milder climates, gardeners can sow seeds early in a cold frame or greenhouse, if they have one. Everyone else has to make do indoors. The best spot is an area out of the path of household traffic. The spot should also be warm and out of drafts. A basement, sun porch, and spare room are all good options. Some people even raise seeds on the tops of dressers, cabinets, or refrigerators!

2. **Provide light.**

   Some seeds germinate under a thin layer of soil mix and some are pressed lightly on top, but in all cases, the seedlings that sprout need between 12 and 16 hours of light per day — that's a lot.

   Sunlight from a window is not at all ideal. It's pale and limited in late winter and early spring. To make your seedlings work, you need artificial light. Fluorescent is best, and a timer at the outlet can help you regulate the hours it's shining on your baby plants.

3. **Prepare pots or flats (which need drainage holes).**

   Begin with sterile seed-starting mix. (This mix is available in bags wherever gardening supplies are sold.) Fill the containers about three-quarters full with dampened, not drenched, mix (Figure 6-2A). Tamp the surface flat and level with the flat of your hand or a small piece of wood before sowing.

4. **Okay, sow!**

   The back of the seed packet can tell you how
   deep and whether you should cover the seeds
   with mix. The packet can also tell you how far
   apart to place the seeds. Sow carefully by hand —
   a pencil tip is a useful tool when placing small
   seeds (Figure 6-2B).

 Don't sow too many seeds! This overplanting can
   lead to a forest of seedlings, growing too thickly
   for you to thin them without damaging some.

   If you're sowing into a flat, make little furrows
   with the pencil tip or a finger and space the seeds
   up to an inch apart (Figure 6-2C).

5. **Cover.**

   Cover the container the very day you plant.
   Plastic wrap is great, but depending on the size of
   your starting containers, you can instead use a
   plastic bag (Figure 6-2D). This covering holds in
   warmth and humidity, giving the seeds the best
   chance of absorbing moisture and getting going.
   Don't seal too tightly, though. A tight seal causes
   condensed water to drip back down into the mix,
   making things too soggy.

6. **Check back daily.**

   Don't let the planting mix dry out, or the seeds'
   growth will come to a halt. Open the bag a couple
   hours every few days to let the soil breathe some
   fresh air. Then close it back up. The best way to
   keep developing seedlings evenly, consistently
   moist is with bottom watering. Just set the container into a few inches of water (in the sink or a
   tray) and let it wick up the water it needs before
   returning the container to its spot.

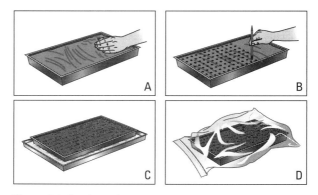

Figure 6-2: Seed-starting trays.

The first little seeds usually take a week or two to poke up their heads. But what a thrill! Here's what to do now to ensure that they survive and thrive:

🖝 **Snip away extras.** Use tiny scissors (fingernail or beard-clipping ones work well) to gently cut weaker seedlings away at soil level. Pulling rather than cutting off can damage the roots of the surrounding seedlings. The properly spaced survivors gain better air circulation, and their developing roots don't have to compete for precious resources.

🖝 **Water from above with a fine spray.** As the seedlings grow bigger, bottom watering may no longer be practical. You can shift the flat's plastic covering on and off for ventilation — after a while, the young plants become too tall, and you have to remove it completely.

✔ **Start fertilizing.** A diluted, half-strength flowering-houseplant fertilizer delivered with a regular watering is just fine. Fertilize about every two weeks.

✔ **Check that the seedlings are well-rooted when they're several inches high.** Never tug on the stem! Gently tug on the true leaves (not the first, or *cotyledon,* leaves that come up). If the seedlings hang on and otherwise look husky, they're ready to get hardened off (see the next section).

Planting transplants in the garden

Regardless of whether you grow your transplants yourself or purchase them from a supplier, the first step toward getting them into the ground is the hardening-off process. This interim step eases them from their plush indoor life to the realities of life in the real world — outdoors in the garden.

After the threat of frost has passed, move your seedlings outside to a place that's sheltered from sun and wind. Start with an hour a day, and gradually work it up to 24 hours over a two-week period. (Bring the seedlings indoors or cover them on chilly nights or if frost threatens.) Stop fertilizing them. If you bought your transplants from somewhere else, you may be able to shorten this process by asking the seller whether they were hardened off.

When the seedlings are hardened off, you're to get the seedlings off to a good start. Ideally, work on an overcast day (or plant late in the day) when the hot sun won't stress them or you. Here's what to do:

1. **Water the seedlings well the morning you plan to plant.**

2. **Dig individual holes.**

   The holes should be at least as deep and wide as the pot the seedling comes in. How far apart to dig depends on the plant. The tag that comes with should have this information, but when in doubt, allow more elbow room rather than less.

3. **Pop each plant out of its pot carefully, handling the seedlings by gently gripping the leaves.**

   Tease apart the roots on the sides and bottom so they'll be more inclined to enter the surrounding soil in their new home. Place the roots gently in their hole and tamp the soil in around them firmly to eliminate air pockets.

    You can plant tomato seedlings deeper than they were growing in their pot; in other words, you can bury much of the stem with no harm done; just keep one or two sets of leaves above ground and gently remove the lower ones. Not only does this planting depth lead to better stability in the hole, but the stem also responds by making more roots along the buried part.

4. **Water, then mulch.**

   Gently soak each seedling quite well, using a wand attachment on your hose or a watering can. Then lay down an inch or two of mulch an inch out from the base of each seedling and outward to conserve soil moisture as well as to thwart sprouting weeds. Don't let the mulch touch the stem, or you risk insect and pest problems later on.

    Offer a little protection. Sudden exposure to sun and wind can stress out little plants. Get them through the first few days by setting some boxes or boards nearby to create a barrier — or set a few lawn chairs out in the garden over the seedlings. It helps.

Sowing seeds directly into the garden

All danger of frost is past, the air and soil have warmed up, and the ground is slightly damp or even somewhat dry. In other words, it's very late spring or early summer, and you're ready to sow your seeds.

Assuming that the garden area is prepared and ready to go, head outdoors one fine day with seed packets, a trowel, a planting dibble or hoe (depending on the size of the project), and something to sit on. Follow these steps:

1. **Make planting holes or furrows.**

   Recommended planting distances are noted on the seed packets.

2. **Follow the "three friends" rule — plant three seeds per hole.**

   At least one will likely sprout well. If all three do, you can thin out two of them later to favor the most robust one.

3. **Cover each hole as you go, tamping down the soil to eliminate air pockets.**

4. **Label.**

   The now-empty seed packet, stapled to a small stick, is a long-time labeling favorite, but you can simply write the name of the vegetable (and variety if you're growing more than one of the same kind) as well as the date on a stick with a marker and plunge it in at the head of the row.

5. **Water well with a soft spray so you don't dislodge the seeds.**

   A wand hose attachment is good, as is a watering can with a rose head. If your vegetable garden is fairly big, use a sprinkler.

6. **Mulch.**

   Lay down an inch or two of mulch after watering over the entire bed; keep the mulch an inch away from your new planting so that the seeds don't have to try to get through the barrier. Mulching conserves soil moisture and discourages sprouting weeds.

Chapter 7

Live Long and Prosper: Giving Plants What They Need

. . . .

In This Chapter

▶ Letting in enough light

▶ Figuring out fertilizer, compost, and mulch

▶ Testing for and adjusting pH

▶ Getting the right amount of water

. . . .

*W*hen you properly prepare the foundation of your garden, making sure plants can get what they need, success follows. The formula's as simple as that.

The needs of plants aren't weird or complicated, but you may find that if you omit any of the recommendations in this chapter — either on purpose or unintentionally — trouble can follow. So consider this chapter a bit of a checklist as you get your garden ready for growing! Ready? Here you go. The work you do now can save you a lot of effort later.

Improving a bed or area prior to planting is so much easier than doing so after. Do these tasks early if you can.

Let There Be Light!

Every plant needs at least some light in order to grow and prosper, but the amount really varies. Mushrooms (which are actually fungi), for instance, can grow in bins in a dim basement or shed; daisies and waterlilies, on the other hand, crave hot, full-on sunshine. Plenty of plants rest in the middle of these two extremes, of course. And some plants, like azaleas and day lilies, grow well enough in less-optimum light but don't flower well in the shade. In terms of labeling, just remember that *full sun* usually means six or more hours per day; *part-day,* of course, refers to less.

For a plant to operate, thrive, and increase in size, all plant parts (except flowers) need to play their roles in photosynthesis. Roots draw in water, but the real energy production takes place primarily in the foliage. Light helps produce the fuel.

Long hours of plentiful sunlight, with varying angles throughout the day, are important so that every leaf — even the ones lower down on the plant — gets the chance to receive light. The good news is that no matter what light conditions your yard has to offer, at least something should be able to grow there. Sun plants and shade plants are labeled, and of course gardeners try to accommodate them.

The warmth of the sun, even more than actual light, inspires flowers to unfurl. Sunlight from the east (morning light) is considered cooler, and western sun (afternoon light) can be scorching. Many plants prefer a site with some morning sun, even until midday, and late-afternoon shade. Other plants are able to endure even the hottest conditions. A plant's tolerance, of course, varies by region.

If you have plants growing in a spot that receives a blast of late-afternoon sun, monitor their water needs closely so they don't dry out. If you find they're struggling, install something to cast a shadow, such as an arbor, or plant a tree or large shrub in just the right spot. Even companion perennials or annuals planted nearby can cast enough shade to bring needed relief.

Here are signs that a plant is getting too much sun:

- ✔ Flower petals dry out.
- ✔ Leaf edges look burnt or dried.
- ✔ Flower color looks faded or washed out.
- ✔ The entire plant starts to flag.

Here are signs that a plant isn't getting enough light:

- ✔ Growth is sparse.
- ✔ Stems are lanky and spindly.
- ✔ The distance between leaves, where they're attached to the stems, is especially wide.
- ✔ You see fewer flower buds and, thus, fewer flowers.
- ✔ The entire plant leans toward the light sources.

Some of figuring out the proper location is trial and error — you're aware that roses like a full day of sun, but you really want that bush to go in the nook that gets afternoon shade. Give the spot a try. If the plant's unhappy, you can always move it.

Facing the Fertilizer Facts

Fertilizing — that is, supplying your plants with supplemental minerals — is an important part of gardening. A well-timed dose of fertilizer really boosts a plant. You can't argue with success!

Just as a healthy diet allows a person or animal to prosper, so does a good and appropriate supply of nutrients keep a plant healthy and happy. Plants have complex systems in need of chemicals to help them produce their own foods. The three primary plant-growth elements, or nutrients, are as follows:

- ✔ **N (nitrogen):** Enhances stem and leaf growth (for most plants, nitrogen ends up being the most important nutrient)

- ✔ **P (phosphorus):** Contributes to flower production, fruit production, seed production, and root growth

- ✔ **K (potassium):** Ensures general vigor; helps plants resist disease

An all-purpose, balanced formulation contributes to overall plant health. These top three nutrients are usually listed on the back labels of bags of fertilizer that you can buy in any garden supply store. They're usually listed in order as numbers on the package (N-P-K). A *balanced* fertilizer (one that contains the three most important elements — nitrogen, phosphorus, and potassium) may show up as 5-10-5 or even 5-10-10. You can find are plenty of other variations, depending on the intended use of the fertilizer.

A fertilizer label often tells you which kind of fertilizer is best for your particular garden. If in doubt about your garden's needs, talk to someone at your local garden nursery or supply store.

Certain plants demand more or less of the top three nutrients. But most garden flowers are not specialists, which is why generally fertile soil is desirable and why all-purpose fertilizer is most commonly recommended.

Good soil also contains secondary nutrients, like calcium, magnesium, and sulfur, as well as some trace elements, called *micronutrients,* that enhance plant health and growth. You usually don't have to add these nutrients to the soil. However, soil tests sometimes indicate that gardeners should add micronutrients or secondary nutrients, especially calcium (see "Finding out your soil's pH" for info on soil tests).

Fertilizing good soil is often optional. If you have fertile, organically rich soil, many of your plants may do just fine without it — particularly if you develop the habit of amending the soil regularly (once or twice a year) with more organic matter. If your garden soil is organically rich, it's fertile and thus should have the major elements. If not, or if you're pushing your plants to peak performance, you can use plant food or fertilizer, natural or organic, to supply or supplement these important nutrients.

 Constantly fertilizing lousy soil isn't a good idea. Not only is it a lot of work and expense for you, but it's also a losing battle. Salts build up, plants are never really healthy in the long term, and the soil texture remains poor. You're far better off increasing the organic matter and just using fertilizer as a nutrient boost for your plants — if they need it. *Organic matter* — once-living material that releases nutrients as it decays — includes compost, dehydrated manure, chopped leaves, damp peat moss, and ground-up bark.

Depending on what you use, how much, the plant in question, and so forth, the effects of adding fertilizer can be impressive. But they're not instant. Wait two weeks to a month before assessing the results.

"Feed the soil, not the plants!" is an old gardening adage, and these are words to live by, folks. You can't go wrong taking the time and effort to build up soil fertility and structure at least once a year, more often if the opportunity presents itself. Dig in organic matter, add it to every planting hole (except when planting trees and shrubs), *top-dress* (sprinkle some on the soil surface at planting time), and *side-dress* (deliver more over the root zone midseason).

Most plants like to be fertilized at planting time, just to get off to a good start. Thereafter, you may fertilize again on a monthly basis. Reduce or stop when fall's cooler weather arrives. Fertilizer inspires fresh new growth, and you don't want that then — fall is a time for plants to slow down and approach dormancy, and cold weather can damage new growth.

If you're using store-bought or chemical fertilizer, read the label to figure out how to deliver the fertilizer and how much to use. Some fertilizers work best if you dig them right into the soil; others are better delivered in dilute form when you water. The label can also tell you how much to use per square foot of garden area and how often to apply. For bagged organic fertilizer, read the label; otherwise, do some research on your own.

More is not better! (Though if you're fertilizing with compost, using too much is almost impossible — see the next section.) Plant fertilizer is like aspirin. The right amount is beneficial; too

much is harmful. So don't get carried away.
Some fertilizers are types of salt, and high con-
centrations of any salt can kill plants. Always
read the label and follow the directions carefully. To get the amounts right, you may have to
pull out the tape measure and figure out how
many square feet of garden you need to cover.

Some gardeners like to fertilize their plants half
as much, twice as often. That's perfectly okay.
Just make sure you dilute properly and get your
measurements right.

Compost: More than Just a Fertilizer

I talk about compost in the fertilizer section, but
compost is useful and necessary to your garden in
so many ways other than as plain fertilizer. Because
it's organically rich, with good texture, compost is
just about the best thing you can add to soil. What
works best depends on the type and fertility of your
native soil, but you can't go wrong digging in quite a
lot of compost. Compost lightens clay soil and gives
needed substance to sandy soil. Less-extreme soils
can still benefit.

Don't use soggy or overly dry compost.
Compost should be fully decayed, dark in
color and crumbly in texture. This issue is
more significant with homemade compost than
the bagged, store-bought sort. For homemade,
you're fine if you take it from the bottom of the
pile (most store-bought composters have a
convenient hatch there).

Whether you're planting a young perennial or a bunch of annuals, always dig a hole both deeper and wider than the root ball. This practice gives you an opportunity to make an area the roots can eagerly expand into. Either scoop some compost into the bottom of the hole (where a lot of root growth should occur) or mix compost with the native soil (try a 50-50 mix).

In general, potted plants like a lighter medium. Go ahead and put a handful or two of compost in along with the potting soil, but don't be heavy-handed.

Quite a few gardeners make their own compost, a process that can take three months to a year to complete. Many gardeners use a compost bin for this process, though you can just pile the compost in an isolated and sectioned-off portion of your yard. Your compost pile should be kept slightly damp but not soggy. Stirring or turning the material every few weeks can speed up the decomposition process. When the compost is dark brown, is cool to the touch, and has a pleasant "earthy" smell, it's ready to use.

Good material choices for mixing and making your own compost include

- ✔ Chopped-up leaves
- ✔ Any young weeds that have *not* gone to seed
- ✔ Old lettuce or other salad greens
- ✔ Prunings from healthy plants

Don't compost weeds that have gone to seed, any diseased plants, or any plants that have been sprayed with herbicides. Also, animal fats or spoiled meat are not recommended and often attract rodents.

Demystifying Soil pH

The *pH* (and you can find various arguments about exactly what pH stands for) is the measure of your soil's acidity. Too low of a soil pH means the soil's too acidic, and too high of a pH means the soil is alkaline. Generally speaking, you want your soil pH to be on the *slightly* acidic side for the vast majority of garden plants. Extremes are rarely good. The pH scale ranges from acidic to alkaline — 0 to 14, with 7.0 as neutral. The really good news is that many soils are fairly close to neutral.

Acidic or alkaline soil isn't bad soil or bad for plant growth per se. But the minerals in the soil that are important to plant growth and health have a tough time getting to the plants when the pH isn't right for the particular plant. Scientists have discovered that beneficial soil bacteria don't function well unless the soil pH is relatively close to neutral. These bacteria are important because they break down organic matter and make sure nutrients are in forms that plants can use.

Of course, some plants prefer or are well-adapted to pH levels that are a little more acidic or a little more alkaline. And some soils are naturally so; when in doubt, you can take your cue from the native plants.

Examples of plants that like acidic soil include blueberries, azaleas, rhododendrons, most other broadleaf evergreens, and heather. Examples of plants that like alkaline soil include penstemon, dianthus, baby's breath, and beets.

Finding out your soil's pH

You can do a little detective work by observing which native plants are thriving and then confirming that they have a preference one way or another. Or you can run a soil test — use either an inexpensive kit or arrange one of those more-intense tests where you take soil samples from various parts of your yard and mail the dirt in to a lab. The nice thing about doing this more-intense test is that the lab report not only tells you the pH but also gives you recommendations on how to improve or alter your soil. Check with your local Cooperative Extension Service — workers there may be able to run the tests for you at a minimal cost.

Adjusting your soil's pH

Of course you can adjust your soil's pH! Gardeners do it all the time when they know their lot in life is extreme soil, or even when they're just trying to please some special fussy plant. You just dig in something that nudges the pH in the direction you want it to go:

- ✔ **If your soil is too acidic:** To raise the pH, dig in dolomitic limestone, bonemeal, or wood ashes. How much? I knew you were going to ask that! The answer has to do with how much ground you want to alter or improve. If you really need to adjust the pH, I strongly recommend you get that lab-analyzed soil test, because the lab can give you good, tailored directions on what to do and how much amendment(s) to add. Just so you know, though, the general rule of thumb for adding granulated limestone is between 5 and 10 pounds per 100 square feet of garden area.

- ✔ **If your soil is too alkaline:** To lower the pH, dig in some acidic organic matter such as peat moss, sawdust, well-chopped leaves from oak trees, or pine needles. Alternatively, you can add calcium sulfate, iron sulfate, aluminum sulfate, or powdered sulfur.

If you don't let the sawdust, leaves, or pine needles decompose somewhat before adding them to the soil, they can leach nitrogen from the soil as they break down. And too much peat moss can waterlog the soil as well as make it quite acidic. Consider adding no more than one part of organic amendment to three parts soil. You need professional advice on application rates if you decide to go with powdered sulfur or other additives.

Much Ado about Mulch

Mulch is a good gardening habit but not mandatory. But, ooh boy, do the benefits make it worth the effort! A really good job of mulching your garden usually

✔ Inhibits weed germination and growth (and not only are weeds unsightly, but they also they steal resources from your plants!)

✔ Holds in soil moisture, protecting your plants from drying out so fast

✔ Moderates soil-temperature fluctuations (this benefit is especially valuable during that turbulent-weather period in spring when you don't want your plants to be stressed)

✔ In cold-winter areas, protects plant roots from winter cold and helps prevent *frost-heaving,* in which plants are literally pushed out of the ground by the natural expansion and contraction of the soil as it cools off and heats up

✔ In hot-summer areas, helps keep plant roots cooler

✔ Depending on what you use, adds a bit of welcome nutrition to your garden as it breaks down

Sound like good enough reasons to use mulch? Yeah, I thought I'd convince you. Read on for more on mulches.

Knowing your mulches

First of all, I can't name any "right" or "best" mulch. Benefits vary in different climates and parts of the country. Some mulches are free, right in your own backyard; you can purchase others locally. Experiment to find out what you and your plants prefer. Table 7-1 provides the basic information you need to know about some of the more popular options.

Table 7-1	Comparing Mulching Options	
Type of Mulch	Advantages	Concerns
Grass clippings	Is cheap, readily available, and easy to apply	Decays quickly, so you have to replenish it often; if you use weed killers on your lawn or nitrogen-heavy fertilizer, it may adversely affect other parts of the garden; can turn slimy if you apply more than an inch or so at a time; if the grass went to seed before you cut it, the grass seeds can germinate in your garden beds (yikes!)

Type of Mulch	Advantages	Concerns
Wood or bark chips	Looks neat and attractive; stays where you put it; is slow to decay	Pine bark mulch is fairly acidic, which you may or may not want for your garden; if you apply too deeply (over 3") or apply a deep layer up against tree and shrub trunks, you may create a hiding spot for a bark-damaging rodent, especially during winter
Decaying leaves	Smothers weeds very well; helps hold in soil moisture	Is not especially attractive; if it contains seeds, they can germinate and become a weed problem; if the leaves are soft, like maple leaves, the mulch can mat; if it's acidic (oak especially), it can lower your garden soil's pH
Compost	Is free and plentiful if you have your own compost pile; adds nutrients to the soil as it breaks down	Makes a good place for weeds to take hold; fresh compost (especially if it contains manure or grass clippings) can burn plants
Peat moss	Looks neat and tidy; is versatile — also functions as a soil amendment	Can be expensive; if dry, will repel water; becomes crusty over time

(continued)

Table 7-1 *(continued)*

Type of Mulch	Advantages	Concerns
Straw	Is cheap and easy to apply	Is so light it can blow or drift away; may harbor rodents, especially over the winter months; isn't very attractive for ornamental plantings
Hay	Is cheap and easy to apply	May harbor rodents, especially over the winter months; isn't very attractive for ornamental plantings; probably contains weed seeds!
Gravel, pebbles, or stone	Has a nice, neat look (though not "natural"); is easy to apply; won't wash away easily and will last a long time; doesn't need to be replenished over the course of a season in colder climates	Can allow weeds to sneak through; provides no benefits to the soil
Plastic (garden plastic, black plastic)	Keeps weeds at bay; holds soil moisture and warmth in	Watering and feeding is hard (you need to cut openings for plants); can be difficult to apply unless you're doing an entire area at one time; isn't very attractive

How to apply mulch

Here's what you need to know to ensure you get the best possible use of your mulch:

- ✔ **When you plant:** Applying mulch right after planting something is easy. Use a shovel or scoop with a trowel. Spread the mulch over the root-zone area but not flush up against a plant's base or main stem (which can smother it or invite pests or disease). Depth depends on the sort of plant. Annuals and perennials are fine with an inch or so of mulch.

- ✔ **During the growing season:** Add more mulch midway through the growing season or whenever you notice it's depleted. You may have to get down on your knees or wriggle around a bit as you try to deliver it where it's needed without harming the plant or its neighbors. Again, use less for smaller plants, more for bigger ones.

- ✔ **In the fall or for winter protection:** Depending on the severity of your winters and the amount of snow cover you expect, you want to cover an overwintering plant well. You can cut down perennials first and then practically bury them under several inches of mulch.

 These amounts are guidelines only. You have to tailor them to your climate, growing season, and specific plants.

Tackling Watering Issues

Sure, without moisture, plants die. Everyone knows that. But you may not know why water is so incredibly vital. The answer is threefold, actually:

✔ Sufficient water pressure within plant tissues creates *turgor,* or rigidity, so the plant can stand up. A plant without turgor pressure collapses.

✔ Water keeps nutrients flowing through the soil, the roots, and the plant parts as they should.

✔ The show is the chemical process of photosynthesis, which you no doubt remember from biology class in school. The plant uses light, carbon dioxide, and water to make sugar (a pretty impressive trick). Without photosynthesis, plants can't grow or develop flowers or fruit.

The following sections tell you what you need to know about watering.

Providing plants with the right amount of moisture

How do you make sure your garden has the right amount of moisture? Relying on natural rainfall would be nice, but natural rainfall is hard to count on. You just need to keep an eye on things and pay attention to your plants. Read on for the signs of too much or too little water.

On the dry side

If you know what to look for, you can figure out your plants' watering needs. Plants actually prioritize when water-stressed, so look for the early warning signs:

1. **If a plant isn't getting enough water, flower petals and buds are the first things to be jettisoned (or fruit if it has developed), because making and maintaining them takes so much energy and water.**

2. **Next to go are the leaves, which shrivel.**

3. **Then the stems flop.**

4. **Underground, the roots go limp.**

Obviously, if your garden is in this condition, it needs more water.

Bogged down

Telling when a plant doesn't have enough water may seem to be a snap, but keep in mind that there's definitely such a thing as too much water. If puddles form in your garden or an area of it's quite soggy, all the pores in the soil fill. When this happens, no free oxygen, which needs to get to the roots, is in the soil.

Meanwhile, some plant diseases (like mildew and blight) travel via water and can easily develop and spread in soaked conditions. Sodden roots blacken and rot, and all the aboveground growth subsequently dies. Garden plants in these circumstances, of course, need less water. See "Dealing with drainage problems" later in this chapter to find out what to do.

Unfortunately, an overwatered plant looks the same as one that's underwatered! The reason is that an overwatered plant is actually suffering from dehydration because the roots have been damaged by too much water (actually, too little oxygen, because the water has displaced the oxygen); the roots can't absorb water, so the plant wilts. One difference is that overwatered plants don't recover from wilt when you apply additional water, but underwatered ones generally do.

Determining which watering system to use

The amount of water your garden needs depends on what kind of soil you're using, what your climate is like, and what kinds of plants you have. Shallow-rooted plants need more water than deep-rooted ones because they're closer to the soil surface, which dries out more quickly in the heat of the sun. Deep roots can reach the more consistently damp lower soil layers.

For many gardeners, getting enough water to their gardens is the biggest gardening challenge. If you're crunched for time or have a large area to water, installing in-ground sprinklers and irrigation systems may be a good idea. Employing the use of a regular watering system, such as drip irrigation or an in-ground system, is the best approach to ensuring a consistent moisture cycle to grow happy, healthy plants. However, in-ground watering systems tend to be expensive and should be installed by professionals.

Of course, you can always water your garden your-self, by hand, and really that's a great way to do it, because you can personally inspect each plant. For details about equipment like soaker hoses and porta-ble sprinklers to help you with your watering, check out Chapter 4.

Whether you water by hand or use a system, here are some things you may want to keep in mind:

- ✔ Watering your garden early in the morning, before the sun is fully overhead, is usually best. Watering at night can make plants susceptible to diseases that cause them to rot.

- ✔ Some plants in your garden, such as melons, may require more water than others, in which case watering by hand is probably best.

- ✔ Usually, watering the soil rather than the leaves is best because the roots are what absorb water, and they're in the soil. Also, wetting the

leaves can result in more disease problems.
Still, on a very hot or windy day, watering the
leaves can reduce wilt and lower leaf
temperatures.

✔ Unless you have a very large garden, sprinkler
heads that you attach to garden hoses are usually better suited for lawns than gardens. If you
decide to use one, make sure the sprinkler
covers the entire garden area evenly and
doesn't water things you don't want watered,
like your lawn furniture.

✔ No matter what kind of garden you have or
which watering system you use, infrequent deep
soakings are better than frequent shallow
waterings.

Cutting back on watering

Even if you don't live in an area experiencing
drought, you don't want to waste water, no matter
what you pay for it or how much you have to use.
Remember that for most efficient delivery, water in
early to mid-morning — after the dew has dried but
before the heat of the day sets in and much of the
water evaporates. And mulch, mulch, mulch individual plants and entire beds to hold in the water right
by the roots, where plants most need and appreciate
it. I go into more detail about mulch earlier in this
chapter in "Much Ado about Mulch."

Wherever possible, build up a basin of
mounded-up dirt or mulch around the edge of
the rootball of each plant at planting time.
Water goes right in the basin and soaks directly
down into the root system instead of running off
onto the lawn or driveway or elsewhere where it
isn't needed.

The method of delivery can also save water: In-ground irrigation systems are wonderfully efficient, as I mention earlier in this chapter; soaker hoses are also good. Drip systems shouldn't produce any appreciable runoff on slopes. And although some sprinklers are good, others are wasteful. Check out mail-order catalogs that specialize in types of sprinklers. They're filled with good information on how to choose the right ones.

Rain gauges are useful for measuring water when you apply it with overhead sprinklers. For drip systems, run them for an hour or two and then dig down into the soil around the plant to see how far down and wide the moisture has penetrated. Run the system longer if it hasn't yet penetrated deep enough to reach the root zone. After you do this exercise a few times, you should know how long to run the system each time you water.

Another way to cut back on the amount of watering you need to do is to use drought-tolerant plants in your garden. Gardeners in the Southwestern portion of the United States are particularly good at this type of gardening, largely through necessity. Drought-tolerant plants include cacti, succulents, ceanothus, rock rose, native dryland plants and their cultivars (such as penstemon and gaura), and deep-rooted perennials like prairie natives and their cultivars (such as baptisia, liatris, black-eyed Susans, and purple coneflowers).

Dealing with drainage problems

You know you have a drainage problem in your garden when heavy or even moderate rain leaves puddles that take forever to drain. Or you may find out, to your dismay, that under a few inches of okay soil in your yard is a stubborn layer of *hardpan* (most people discover this water-resistant barrier — often packed clay — when they dig a deeper-than-usual hole, say, for planting a big shrub or a tree).

Really damp areas (especially in humid periods or in shady spots) are slow to evaporate water, whether from rain or from your sprinkler. Then plant diseases can get begin, particularly on foliage. The answer here is to try to improve the air circulation: Prune overhanging growth and give individual plants more elbow room. And when you're in charge of watering, supply it to the roots instead of allowing it to splash the entire plant.

 Obviously, bad drainage isn't good for any garden plant, not just trees and shrubs. If you're smart or lucky, you can deal with the problem before you plant or redo an area. Here are some options, from the simple to the high-tech:

- ✔ **Try improving the soil.** Dig in lots of organic matter. Soil with high organic-matter content allows excess moisture to drain through while absorbing needed water. Sounds paradoxical, but it's true. (Check out the earlier section "Compost: More than Just a Fertilizer.")

- ✔ **Build and garden in raised beds.** You control the soil within, and thus it drains well and your plants are happy. Problem averted.

- ✔ **Create a rain garden or a bog garden, and plant only water-loving plants.** These plants include maples, willows, astilbe, ferns, filipendula, beebalm, mint, various sorts of irises, and canna.

- ✔ **Route water flow away from the garden area.** Just get out there with a trowel or shovel and create some diversion channels. Of course, you don't want to send the problem to another important part of the yard or foist unwanted, excess water on your neighbor. Send it down the driveway and on into the street, or into the gutter. This water needs to head for the storm drains. (If this plan isn't practical, dig a hole nearby, fill it with gravel, and route the channel there.)

✔ **Make a gravel channel.** Follow the advice about rerouting water flow, but dig the channel deeper and fill it with crushed gravel or pebbles. You can hide it from view for some or all of its length by scooping a little soil over it. It'll still do its job of slowly but surely taking the water away.

✔ **Use perforated plastic pipes, lightly or deeply buried, to divert the water to where you want it to go.** Home supply stores sell pipes specifically for this purpose. These pipes usually come in various forms and sizes of plastic.

✔ **If the problem is severe and you can't seem to solve it, drainage tiles, a French drain, or a curtain drain are options.** Installing one of these systems can be a very expensive and involved process. Hire someone experienced to advise you, explain the options, and install.

Apple & Macs

iPad For Dummies,
2nd Edition
978-1-118-02444-7

iPhone For Dummies,
5th Edition
978-1-118-03671-6

iPod touch For Dummies,
3rd Edition
978-1-118-12960-9

Mac OS X Lion
For Dummies
978-1-118-02205-4

Blogging & Social Media

CityVille For Dummies
978-1-118-08337-6

Facebook For Dummies,
4th Edition
978-1-118-09562-1

Mom Blogging
For Dummies
978-1-118-03843-7

Twitter For Dummies,
2nd Edition
978-0-470-76879-2

WordPress
For Dummies,
4th Edition
978-1-118-07342-1

Business

Cash Flow For Dummies
978-1-118-01850-7

Investing For Dummies,
6th Edition
978-0-470-90545-6

Job Searching
with Social Media
For Dummies
978-0-470-93072-4

QuickBooks 2011
For Dummies
978-0-470-64649-6

Resumes For Dummies,
6th Edition
978-0-470-87361-8

Starting an Etsy Business
For Dummies
978-0-470-93067-0

Cooking & Entertaining

Cooking Basics
For Dummies, 4th Edition
978-0-470-91388-8

Wine For Dummies,
4th Edition
978-0-470-04579-4

Diet & Nutrition

Kettlebells For Dummies
978-0-470-59929-7

Nutrition For Dummies,
5th Edition
978-0-470-93231-5

Restaurant Calorie
Counter For Dummies,
2nd Edition
978-0-470-64405-8

Digital Photography

Digital SLR Cameras &
Photography
For Dummies, 4th Edition
978-1-118-14489-3

Digital SLR Settings
& Shortcuts
For Dummies
978-0-470-91763-3

Photoshop Elements 9
For Dummies
978-0-470-87872-9

Gardening

Gardening Basics
For Dummies
978-0-470-03749-2

Vegetable Gardening
For Dummies,
2nd Edition
978-0-470-49870-5

Green/Sustainable

Raising Chickens
For Dummies
978-0-470-46544-8

Green Cleaning
For Dummies
978-0-470-39106-8

Health

Diabetes
For Dummies,
3rd Edition
978-0-470-27086-8

Food Allergies
For Dummies
978-0-470-09584-3

Living Gluten-Free
For Dummies,
2nd Edition
978-0-470-58589-4

Hobbies

Beekeeping
For Dummies,
2nd Edition
978-0-470-43065-1

Chess For Dummies,
3rd Edition
978-1-118-01695-4

Drawing For Dummies,
2nd Edition
978-0-470-61842-4

eBay For Dummies,
7th Edition
978-1-118-09806-6

Knitting
For Dummies,
2nd Edition
978-0-470-28747-7

Language &
Foreign Language

English Grammar
For Dummies,
2nd Edition
978-0-470-54664-2

French For Dummies,
2nd Edition
978-1-118-00464-7

German For Dummies,
2nd Edition
978-0-470-90101-4

Spanish Essentials
For Dummies
978-0-470-63751-7

Spanish For Dummies,
2nd Edition
978-0-470-87855-2

Math & Science

Algebra I For Dummies,
2nd Edition
978-0-470-55964-2

Biology For Dummies,
2nd Edition
978-0-470-59875-7

Chemistry For Dummies,
2nd Edition
978-1-1180-0730-3

Geometry For Dummies,
2nd Edition
978-0-470-08946-0

Pre-Algebra Essentials
For Dummies
978-0-470-61838-7

Microsoft Office

Excel 2010 For Dummies
978-0-470-48953-6

Office 2010 All-in-One
For Dummies
978-0-470-49748-7

Office 2011 for Mac
For Dummies
978-0-470-87869-9

Word 2010
For Dummies
978-0-470-48772-3

Music

Guitar For Dummies,
2nd Edition
978-0-7645-9904-0

Clarinet For Dummies
978-0-470-58477-4

iPod & iTunes
For Dummies, 9th Edition
978-1-118-13060-5

Pets

Cats For Dummies,
2nd Edition
978-0-7645-5275-5

Dogs All-in-One
For Dummies
978-0470-52978-2

Saltwater Aquariums
For Dummies,
2nd Edition
978-0-470-06805-2

Religion & Inspiration

The Bible For Dummies
978-0-7645-5296-0

Catholicism
For Dummies,
2nd Edition
978-1-118-07778-8

Spirituality For Dummies,
2nd Edition
978-0-470-19142-2

Self-Help &
Relationships

Happiness For Dummies
978-0-470-28171-0

Overcoming Anxiety
For Dummies,
2nd Edition
978-0-470-57441-6

Seniors

Crosswords For Seniors
For Dummies
978-0-470-49157-7

iPad For Seniors
For Dummies, 2nd Edition
978-1-118-03827-7

Laptops & Tablets
For Seniors
For Dummies,
2nd Edition
978-1-118-09596-6

Smartphones & Tablets

BlackBerry
For Dummies, 5th Edition
978-1-118-10035-6

Droid X2 For Dummies
978-1-118-14864-8

HTC ThunderBolt
For Dummies
978-1-118-07601-9

MOTOROLA XOOM
For Dummies
978-1-118-08835-7

Sports

Basketball For Dummies,
3rd Edition
978-1-118-07374-2

Football For Dummies,
4th Edition
978-1-118-01261-1

Golf For Dummies,
4th Edition
978-0-470-88279-5

Test Prep

ACT For Dummies,
5th Edition
978-1-118-01259-8

ASVAB For Dummies,
3rd Edition
978-0-470-63760-9

The GRE Test
For Dummies, 7th Edition
978-0-470-00919-2

Police Officer Exam
For Dummies
978-0-470-88724-0

Series 7 Exam
For Dummies
978-0-470-09932-2

Web Development

HTML, CSS, & XHTML
For Dummies, 7th Edition
978-0-470-91659-9

Drupal For Dummies,
2nd Edition
978-1-118-08348-2

Windows 7

Windows 7
For Dummies
978-0-470-49743-2

Windows 7
For Dummies,
Book + DVD Bundle
978-0-470-52398-8

Windows 7 All-in-One
For Dummies
978-0-470-48763-1